SOS TO ROI

A Strategic Approach to Conquer the Complexity Monster and Accelerate Results

LARRY HAAS

INDIE BOOKS
INTERNATIONAL

SOS2ROI® is a registered trademark of Global Aperture Inc.

The Colors of Leadership Time™ is a trademark of Global Aperture Inc.

Three-Stage Planning Process™ is a trademark of Global Aperture Inc.

Now, Next, Monitor™ is a trademark of Global Aperture Inc.

Strategic Improvement Roadmap™ and SIR™ are trademarks of Global Aperture Inc.

ISBN-10: 1-941870-98-8

ISBN-13: 978-1-941870-98-3

Library of Congress Control Number: 2017944867

Designed by Joni McPherson, mcphersongraphics.com

SOS2ROI graphics designed by Claypot Creative, Inc. www.claypotcreative.com

INDIE BOOKS INTERNATIONAL, LLC

2424 VISTA WAY, SUITE 316

OCEANSIDE, CA 92054

www.indiebooksintl.com

Dedication

To Dad.
Thank you for showing me how to be *all in*, and all in *with heart*.
I'll look for you along the trout stream
or in the workshop near the master carpenter.

Table of Contents

SECTION

1

Battling Complexity

CHAPTER 1

The Complexity Monster

Anthony[1] was having an SOS moment.

A likable and seasoned executive, who worked for a large defense firm, Anthony found himself in a precarious spot. His multibillion-dollar military program was not only over budget but also behind schedule, and his customers were beyond livid.

Of the potential performance incentives in the contract, he was receiving exactly none. That is right; zero percent. Things had not been going well for more than a year, and the government was threatening to shut him and his project down, potentially costing billions of dollars in revenue and more than one hundred million dollars in profits for his parent company.

Stressed out, Anthony faced mounting pressure from his bosses and felt micromanaged by his customers. It became increasingly apparent that Anthony's program was in serious need of a rebirth.

The worst day was when Anthony, his bosses, and his entire leadership team were summoned to the Pentagon. Their chief customer, the general, after a stern thirty-minute lecture, exclaimed, "I need to know you care about this program as much as I do. I need to see this mission coursing through every vein in your body—day in and day out—before I can trust you again!"

---

[1] All the stories in this book are inspired by true events. The names and some details have been changed to protect confidentiality.

That's precisely when Anthony experienced what we call an SOS moment.

In 1906, SOS was adopted as the international Morse Code distress signal and is represented by three dots (for *S*), then three dashes (for *O*), followed by another three dots. Although not formally an acronym, SOS in popular usage refers to *Save Our Ship* or *Save Our Souls*, among others.

An SOS moment is a specific instant of keen awareness (understatement coming) that something is fundamentally *not* as it should be.

The next day, Anthony and his bosses asked for assistance from my strategic change management firm. Our team is dedicated to helping companies face these situations, slice through complexity, and forge a path and a plan to accelerate results.

Within hours, and a bit disheveled from their experience, Anthony's team handed over hundreds of documented negative comments from formal feedback reports. They came from members of various related customer entities, along with demands and ideas about how to fix this and that. Over the previous months, his team had been responsive and had tried to act on each item; however, the negativity had kept building. But why?

Working with the program team, we encouraged them to step back and look at the big picture. Instead of reacting to each negative statement, we treated it as a clue to the true root cause of the angst. Working together over a three-month period, we built a twelve-stage plan dubbed the "Path to Excellence."

Initially, the customer team was skeptical. But over time, as

Anthony's team brought them into the process, they recognized that they each (Anthony's team, the parent company, and the customer) had contributed to a negative dynamic, which hampered leadership, stifled productivity, and constrained problem-solving.

Like it or not, they all needed to work together to get out of the mess, not simply blame the problems on Anthony and his team. Embracing the approach, they each committed to implementing their part of the twelve-stage plan as a team under Anthony's leadership.

Within a year, the program was back on track, the customer was thrilled, and was routinely advertising the plan to their bosses. Soon, profits leapt to 70 percent, then 85 percent, and eventually to 100 percent of their contract potential.

Anthony reflected: "Sometimes you need to step back, look above the complexity, and solve the few simple problems that take care of everything else. I'm glad we finally did that."

Enter the Complexity Monster

It is no surprise that modern business and life is complex, and quickly becoming increasingly more so. The financial system is increasingly connected, the geopolitical environment is becoming more tightly coupled, and regulation is an ever-expanding moving target. Moreover, trends in customization, specialization, and personalization are fueling exponential increases in the variety of choices available for purchase (as well as where and how), forcing leaders to scramble.

As a result, public and private institutions are facing an increasingly powerful and growing Complexity Monster that threatens to disrupt the business of getting work done, staying competitive, and thriving. More and more of our organizational systems have gone beyond being just complicated (often detailed yet ultimately predictable); they have become truly complex (often unpredictable).

Like it or not, the Complexity Monster is here to stay. As leaders and managers of increasingly complex organizational and business systems, we need to face that reality head on. And while some advocate merely *coping* with complexity, this book is about *conquering* it. If we don't find a way to conquer the Complexity Monster, it will conquer us.

At the same time, the Complexity Monster is increasing in strength. In their *Harvard Business Review* piece, "Learning to Live with Complexity," Gokce Sargut and Rita McGrath posit that the growth in complexity has largely "resulted from the information technology revolution of the past few decades. Systems that used to be separate are now interconnected and interdependent,

Like it or not, the Complexity Monster is here to stay.

which means that they are, by definition, more complex." They go on to describe three properties that determine the complexity of an environment. "The first, *multiplicity*, refers to the number of potentially interacting elements (in that environment). The second, *interdependence*, relates to how connected those elements are. The third, *diversity*, has to do with the degree of heterogeneity (or sameness of the elements). Thus, the greater (these factors), the greater the complexity." [2]

---

[2] Sargut, Gokce, and Rita McGrath. "Learning to Live with Complexity." *Harvard Business Review.* October 07, 2014. Accessed December 23, 2016. https://hbr.org/2011/09/learning-to-live-with-complexity.

So, What's the Problem?

Complex systems and particularly complex organizations can struggle. The Complexity Monster poses some difficult challenges:

- **The Complexity Monster is difficult to see.** The complex organization or business system is difficult to perceive and extremely difficult, if not impossible, to model. "It's a vantage point problem," describe Sargut and McGrath, wherein no single individual can visualize the entire business system. Experts have applied numerous theories to get around this, which have yielded a degree of success. Chaos theory, complexity theory, biological complex adaptive systems (CAS), and other modern theories and frameworks are shedding light on how to both describe and model the Complexity Monster.

- **It's difficult to predict the Complexity Monster's next move.** By definition, the Complexity Monster is constantly changing, and if it can't be fully comprehended, it is difficult to predict its next move. Often, rare events like SOS moments provide valuable insight into the functioning of the Complexity Monster and force leaders to adapt. Also, when leading complex organizations, experts tell us that unintended consequences are often a key challenge. Because the Complexity Monster does not respond in the way the leader envisioned, the system may react in unintended ways. These can be either positive or negative.

- **It's difficult to know what moves will succeed when the Complexity Monster is around.** If one can neither see it nor predict its next move, it becomes increasingly difficult to take definitive action, with confidence, to combat the Complexity Monster successfully while operating, much less transforming, the organization. Traditional management techniques based on the assumption that the boss knows all, and that the organization is linear in nature and predictable, no longer work. According to David J. Snowden and Mary E. Boone in their *Harvard Business Review* article, "A Leader's Framework for Decision-making": "Leaders who try to impose order in a complex context will fail, but those who set the stage, step back a bit, allow patterns to emerge, and determine which ones are desirable will succeed."[3]

Long-term planning cycles, traditional predictive techniques, a preponderance of lagging data, top-down command and control structures, as well as centralized decision-making are increasingly falling on their face amidst this growing complexity phenomenon.

Conquering the Complexity Monster

So, given the Complexity Monster is difficult to see, predict, and plan for, it must be conquered somehow lest it wreak havoc on the leader's organization and results. For a clue about how to handle these challenges, the complexity conqueror would do well to study one of the greatest conquerors ever.

Alexander III of Macedon, better known as Alexander the Great (356 BCE–323 BCE), was notorious for conquering most of the known world in his day. And while in some conquests the battle was bloody, like against the stubborn city of Tyre, many others

[3] Snowdon, David J., and Mary E. Boone. "A Leader's Framework for Decision Making." *Harvard Business Review.* December 07, 2015. Accessed December 23, 2016. https://hbr.org/2007/11/a-leaders-framework-for-decision-making.

were handled diplomatically or without resistance, such as the conquest of the oft-heralded intellectual and cultural city of Susa.

To the people he conquered, Alexander was often seen more as a liberator from previous harsh rule than as a dictator. Part of his genius, it appears, was to apply a mix of strategies to his conquering quest and then to leverage the assets of the conquered to strengthen his base of power, be it physical infrastructure, tax revenue, or access to supplies and supply lines. Many historians view him as "the great" both for his military genius and his

Often, rare events like SOS moments provide valuable insight into the functioning of the Complexity Monster and force leaders to adapt.

diplomatic skills in handling the various populaces of the regions he conquered. We want to conquer the Complexity Monster in much the same way by employing a variety of techniques based on situation presented. Here are some choices.

▶ REMOVE

Some complexity can be easily identified, and if it isn't value-added, it should be eliminated or destroyed. Even when a process or organization or system is set up simply at the outset, in the infinite quest for clarity, organizations often default to defining things down to the ant's backside, resulting in increased detail and bureaucracy.

If the second law of thermodynamics (conditions naturally devolve from order to chaos) applies to something as simple as this author's teenage sons' bedroom, it most certainly applies to organizations. But a word of warning: when eradicating complexity, like any typical monster or villain, may not really be dead; it might be like Westley in *The Princess Bride*, only "mostly dead." So, make sure to fire an extra shot where it counts and totally destroy the Complexity Monster. Simplify wherever possible,

We want to conquer the Complexity Monster in much the same way by employing a variety of techniques based on the situation presented.

especially in areas where complexity provides no value.

To illustrate this concept: on Anthony's program, we stopped all improvement actions that did not directly support the twelve-stage plan. This significantly reduced the number of such efforts marching in parallel, reduced uncertainty and stress, and freed up time to focus on the most critical enhancements. As a result, the improvement efforts progressed quickly.

REMOVE: *AN AUTOMOTIVE INDUSTRY EXAMPLE*

How often does someone buy a car because of the shape of the muffler? The sound or the look or the performance, yes perhaps, but the shape? Quite unlikely. Yet, if I'm an automotive manufacturer and keep a muffler research and development team fully staffed and funded, that team might invent an array of mufflers where perhaps just one or two different types would suffice. Just because it *can* be created doesn't mean it *should* be. In recent years, automotive manufacturers including Ford, Toyota, Volkswagen, and Fiat-Chrysler have realized they can reduce complexity through standardizing parts and part families that can be designed into their entire fleets. Everything from drivetrain components to airbags to turn signals is up for grabs, and most often opportunities exist in places where customers aren't picky (e.g., mufflers). This significantly reduces complexity.

These and similar moves in other industries have led to serious economic advantages, higher quality, and less costly rework. Yet in parallel, these firms have often maintained the complexity of aesthetics for both vehicle interiors and exteriors as well as the features and functions of the differentiating technology—those things the customer truly values. That leads us to the second option for conquering complexity.

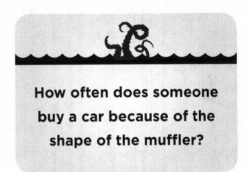

How often does someone buy a car because of the shape of the muffler?

▶ RESTRAIN

While some complexity is within the leader's control and should be removed, other complexity is simply required as part of the business. In these cases, the goal is to lock up the complexity so it doesn't escape and expand beyond its required use. Like a well-tended garden, the issue calls for regular attention. Some firms operate in highly regulated industries where many decision-makers govern the environment. Also, supply-chain structures, product-mix strategies, and the diversity of the organization regarding geographies, reporting structures, and local regulations might require complexity as a necessary evil. The quandary, in these cases, is to decide how much complexity can be tolerated and consciously determine whether to create more complexity in a valuable area of your business. Sometimes, as in the automotive space, a degree of complexity is OK, if not required.

While working on Anthony's program, because we couldn't (by design) reduce the number of organizations (university partners, military customers, suppliers, vendors, etc.), we focused on containing (restraining) the negative impact of this diverse group. One effort emphasized the consistency of program communications in which countless reporting formats are typically used, each customized to a specific organization. Instead, we developed (jointly with the customer) a standard weekly program-tracking briefing that everyone used in the exact same way. Although Anthony's team created it, each program group used it to report vital status to bosses and gain approval for decisions, such as changes to the program technology, investment, or timing. This stemmed the proliferation of innumerable reporting methods and formats and provided the entire team with one *accurate* and *authoritative* status each week.

▶ REINFORCE

The third major option to conquer the Complexity Monster ac-knowledges that some complexity can be valuable, such as in-formal structures that exist between employees. Frequently, or-ganizations ignore this value and leap immediately to "let's just change the organization structure" to alleviate a single difficult issue without considering the benefits of the interdependent re-lationships and mysterious but effective patterns that exist within the current structure.

This "good complexity" exists in great sports teams as well. If one describes a streamlined professional basketball or football offense, much of the excellence is contained in subtle interactions and complexities that exist to enable the no-look pass, the audible, the confidence between quarterback and receiver. They call it "jelling" or "chemistry," and it takes time to develop. As the Irish proverb from the 1500s says,

Some complexity can be valuable, such as informal structures that exist between employees.

"better the devil you know than the devil you don't know." Leaders need to realize that sometimes the Complexity Monster is working for them and take care not to upset the ecosystem producing genuine value.

The complexity in Anthony's program, while a challenge, was also harnessed as a strength. During the initial three-month planning period, we not only worked on the details of the twelve-stage plan, but also on focusing everyone's mindset to be less about typical "police-the-contract" concerns, in which Anthony's team was continually on trial, to more of a focus on "lead together to fulfill the *mission*." This shift fundamentally altered the tone of the daily dialog, nurtured mutual accountability, and cultivated a fresh and broad-based advocacy across the vast program team. As a result, the program's reputation improved, and everyone, regardless of role (soldier, customer, supplier, Anthony's team and parent company, etc.) started winning.

So, in a very real way, the Complexity Monster poses quite a conundrum. While complexity is becoming vastly more prevalent in organizations today, not all of it is bad. As a matter of fact, some complexity can be the source of strength and should be supported.

The Conqueror's Arsenal

The following modern tactics and techniques, which are both prevalent in research and which will be amplified in this book, increase the odds that your organization will be able to succeed in conquering the Complexity Monster, regardless of the method of conquering.

▶ SHORTER PLANNING CYCLES

The days of the ten-year, 100-page strategic plan are fading fast. Plans now span months, or quarters, or even up to a year or two, and should be regularly challenged to see what is working; what assumptions, both internal and external, might be changing; and where adjustments to the plan might be needed. Planning remains critical, but the reliable horizon has changed.

▶ EXPERIMENTATION

Because it's impossible to predict exactly how the Complexity Monster will react, experimentation that is low-cost and high-learning is critical. In their *Harvard Business Review* article, "Experiment with Organizational Change Before Going All In," John Beshears and Francesca Gino expand on the concept of experimentation. They say, "by forcing organizations to articulate their goals clearly and then to rigorously judge their decisions by those metrics, experimental tests can help managers avoid costly mistakes and can open up the consideration of other possible solutions."[4]

▶ COMPLEXITY AS PART OF DECISION CRITERIA

Instead of simply looking at financial and time-based merits of a decision, complexity and its challenges must be put into the mix so managers can take the impact of complexity into

---

[4] Beshears, John, and Francesca Gino. "Experiment with Organizational Change Before Going All In." *Harvard Business Review*. November 06, 2014. Accessed December 28, 2016. https://hbr.org/2014/10/experiment-with-organizational-change-before-going-all-in.

account. If one decides to add complexity, it should be on purpose and for a good reason.

▶ ROUTINE CHALLENGING OF YESTERDAY'S ASSUMPTIONS

The way things work today may or may not be valid tomorrow. Often, assumptions that contribute to a decision are obsolete before the decision is implemented fully. Many recall real-life examples of perfect products designed for yesterday's trends.

▶ DIVERSITY AND COLLABORATION

Like instant replay in sports, a diverse set of eyes and camera angles can yield a much more complete picture of the situation. In organizations, diversity can broadly be seen as the product of experience, cultural background, level in the organization, personality style, thinking skills, or even the ability to perceive, tolerate, and adapt to ambiguity. As a practical matter, taking advantage of the power of this diversity often includes ensuring broad audiences are involved in decision-making, including customers, suppliers, and front-line managers, so the quality of the logic can be maximized. This, of course, requires that the members of the group are confident their perspectives will be heard and that the information they contribute isn't filtered before it gets to the leader. (That is a cultural issue. Much more in the pages ahead.) Done successfully, it can increase the chances of the leader making the right call.

Learning and Adaptability Is Vital

With rapid change and increasing complexity, organizations need to learn how to learn and learn how to adapt. A key mechanism for this is in answering the questions, "What do I need to change?"

and "How do I make that change?" They're not new questions; however, it's in the context of complexity that we want to spend time on them in this book. We believe that by understanding the Complexity Monster and applying the conqueror's arsenal, leaders in today's organizations will be able to confront the challenges punctuated by SOS moments and learn and adapt in a way that can yield a true competitive advantage.

Let's begin the journey.

Chapter 1 Complexity Conqueror's Tactics

- Face the reality that the Complexity Monster is lurking in your organization and is increasing in strength. You will eventually (if not soon) need to conquer this monster.

- Identify areas where organizational complexity exists, is optional, and is not adding any value. Create a plan to reduce or eliminate this complexity (Remove).

- Take stock of those aspects of complexity that are simply part of the business. Then simply acknowledge that's the reality, but don't allow it to expand (Restrain).

- Consider areas where complexity is adding value to the business. Embrace these areas and be careful not to upset the ecosystem that is encouraging that value (Reinforce).

- Continue to expand reliance on the diverse perspectives of those inside and outside your organization who, collectively, may see the complex system much more completely than you. Create a safe environment and culture where those unfiltered perspectives are increasingly accepted, allowing a more complete and accurate picture to form.

CHAPTER 2

The Transformation Process

The Complexity Monster is like a vampire: it sucks the energy and lifeblood out of an organization, making it difficult to move. And, like Bram Stoker's *Dracula*, it doesn't do it all in one bite. No, like death by a thousand paper cuts, its many bites over a span of time are subtle and barely noticed, yet ultimately the victim is left lifeless and drained of essence.

Of course, monsters never think they are monsters. To a monster, its behavior is normal. As linguist, MIT professor, and political commentator Noam Chomsky once opined, "There are very few . . . who are going to look into the mirror and say, ' . . . I see a savage monster. Instead, they make up some construction that justifies what they do."[5] Thus, beginning the quest into the transformation process, one must realize that the Complexity Monster, like many other monsters, may not always appear as a monster at first.

Working on the Business

A common notion expressed across corporate America is that executives should spend more time working "on" the business than "in" it. The "in" part, the daily activity, the core and supporting business processes, etc., are all necessary and should be under continuous improvement to be more productive, and cost-effective.

---

[5] Adams, Tim. "Question Time." Editorial. *The Observer*, November 30, 2003. Accessed April 13, 2017. https://chomsky.info/interviews/20031130/.

Yet the *on* stuff—the major improvements, the strategic changes, the new capabilities, evolving the business, etc.—are efforts that are most often the highest and best use of leadership time, energy, and attention. Although much is written about how to manage individual change initiatives, much less is written on how to become amazing at working *on* the business, making it a natural act, and installing strategic improvement as a core capability. And as the rate of change increases, planning cycles shorten, and organizations become more complex, this capability is both increasingly relevant and timely.

Organizations were increasingly reporting a transformation in outcomes from distress to success.

Any leader can build the organizational capability not only to conquer the Complexity Monster, but also to routinely implement the highest-priority changes that will keep the business at the edge of its competitive max.

Through the years, my team and I have discovered a process that works. This process helps organizations create and implement a high-confidence plan while also addressing current challenges and aligning those charged with implementation. As my firm practiced and refined the approach, we found that organizations were increasingly reporting a transformation in outcomes from distress to success. So, we began to refer to the process as *SOS to ROI (SOS2ROI).*

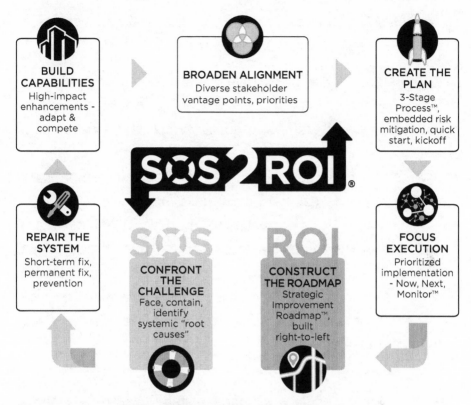

Summary of the SOS2ROI Approach

The following describes the basic steps in the SOS2ROI approach. Often an iterative process, these steps summarize the basic logic applied while moving from distress (SOS) to success in terms of improved return on investment (ROI) in people, time, and dollars.

Each step is illustrated using the analogy of a car.

STEP 1: *CONFRONT THE CHALLENGE*

The process begins with the realization that something is horribly wrong and quick action is needed to limit damage and find the root cause. This often includes a cry for help.

> *Oh no; the car is running rough and making a loud noise* (whoop, whoop, whoop, clank, clank, clank) *and we*

*need to pull over now! The left rear tire has a puncture
and is flat. Do we have a spare?*

This is the SOS moment—the painful and universally inconvenient
realization that things are *not* as they should be. In business, this
might be a broken system (e.g., quality, supply chain, or customer
service issues), or a gap in capabilities (e.g., too inefficient to
match market pricing demands). The actual chilling moment could
be an angry phone call from a top customer or employee, or a
government agency, or internal audit, or an attorney. It could also
come in the form of a consultant report or market analysis showing
declining market share, or a bearish assessment of share price.
Regardless of the source, it's time to go heads-down, limit the
damage, find the root cause, and install at least a temporary fix in
order to resume operations.

STEP 2: *REPAIR THE SYSTEM*

Next, it's time to identify what in the system allowed the issue to
occur in the first place and what in the system needs to change to
prevent the issue from ever occurring again.

*It turns out no one replaced the tires after 40,000 miles.
We need to get a fresh set of tires, be on the lookout
for foreign objects, and from now on only drive on well-
maintained roads.*

Sometimes, issues arise from a flaw in the business system that
needs to be fixed (e.g., supply chain, product design, operations,
or customer service). The challenge is to take the time to create
a repair (often in the form of a change initiative) that prevents
future occurrence. Unfortunately, many organizations rationalize
that since the issue has been resolved (for now), the fix can wait.

Ultimately, they fail to fully install the repair and end up suffering repeated issues as a result.

STEP 3: *BUILD CAPABILITIES*

Next, the process is about looking at what specifically needs to be in place more permanently to take the organization where it wants to go. It's about defining the gap relative to future aspirations and needs.

> *This journey requires we go off-road. How about we upgrade to a set of beefy run-flat tires, so we aren't limited to only the well-maintained roads?*

In some cases, a short-term solution might be needed to bridge capabilities until a more permanent solution can be put in place. At this stage, the leader is identifying the opportunity for improvement and thinking about what the initiative might look like. This effort, like system repairs, includes defining an overall concept, outlining top-level objectives and scope, and identifying the team, budget, and schedule.

STEP 4: *BROADEN ALIGNMENT*

Realizing that most organizations have multiple improvement opportunities, the team responsible for the improvements will need to not only set priorities but also gain alignment with stakeholders around the likely effectiveness of the strategy and elicit their support.

> *Everyone agree that getting run-flat tires makes sense? Do you all think we should do it, and that we can pull it off in time?*

Key considerations, many times in the context of strategic off-site meetings, include what kind of a team they need to become, what success looks like, and what each person is willing to commit to achieve success.

STEP 5: *CREATE THE PLAN*

After gaining agreement on a basic approach and that it's a priority worth pursuing, the team builds a detailed plan, complete with risk mitigation, budgets, and timelines.

> *Let's get those tires in the next month, to make sure they haven't run out of our size.*

Here the key risks are identified, mitigation steps are envisioned, and those steps are wrapped back into the detailed plan. The team understands how it will operate on a daily or weekly basis, how it will measure progress, report status, request help, and make changes to the plan.

STEP 6: *FOCUS EXECUTION*

The perfect solution to the problem with the perfect plan and in perfect priority means little without the drumbeat of daily execution. Many corporate antibodies conspire to knock critical improvements off track, and team members can get distracted with competing priorities, lose focus, or worse—secretly reduce scope to make their lives more manageable.

> *What are we doing today, tomorrow, and the next day to keep focused on ensuring the new tires are shipped, installed and road-tested on time?*

At this stage, it is critical to manage the bandwidth (the collective attention span and degree of focus) of the individual teams. More than money or time, bandwidth is often the limiting element in improvement initiatives. Teams need to learn not to take on too much, but instead to focus and finish what they are doing so that an improvement can complete its implementation, "stick," and yield intended results. Teams need to learn to manage changes so that pressure for scope-creep is exposed and adjustments can be made to ensure priorities stay on track.

STEP 7: *CONSTRUCT THE ROADMAP*

Given many improvement initiatives are usually in play at any one time, it's critical to understand how they all work together.

Knowing that it's bad form and largely ineffective to attempt to implement these all at once, the effective leader uses logic and judgment to lay out a multiquarter improvement plan—a roadmap—with clear priorities, while also pro-

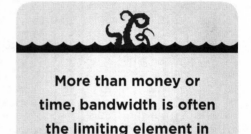

More than money or time, bandwidth is often the limiting element in improvement initiatives.

tecting the bandwidth of the implementation team. Subsequent initiatives are authorized when they are ready, but not before.

> *We will get new tires, then we will repaint the car, then we will get a new driver, and finally, we will install the turbocharger so we can race off-road.*

Often, roadmaps cover a range of opportunities to include improvements in operational systems, development of people, culture, leadership, and new capabilities to enable growth. Many leaders find that the plan becomes clearer over time and that activities become more relevant to stakeholders at all levels.

STEP 8: *MANAGE THE PORTFOLIO*

Once an organization completes the preceding steps once, it

can begin to make periodic corrections to the plan, update the roadmap, build momentum, and incorporate new priorities on a regular basis, based on changing needs and dynamics. As initiatives complete implementation and yield results, bandwidth frees up to address emerging priorities.

Since these tires worked out so great, why don't we put the car on a regular maintenance program? And while we're at it, let's add the RV and the motorcycle, too.

Organizations that learn to stop and freeze lower-priority projects, defend priorities, and continually manage the bandwidth of the leadership team typically find the greatest ROI in people, time, and dollars.

Where We Are Going: *Advice for Using this Book*

Section II of this book will cover the first seven steps of the SOS2ROI transformation in more detail, while Section III will focus on step eight—managing transformation success. At any given time, you may find yourself in the middle of the process, and that's OK. Look up the chapter that is most relevant to where you are that day and bring in the rest as needed. Remember, there are often iterations during the initial pass-through and even tweaks as experience reveals hidden issues.

A Caveat: *This Is Not a Strategic Encyclopedia*

There are many ways to set up an organizational strategic framework. And no matter how you do it, the SOS2ROI approach can work inside of it. To illustrate, at the time of this book's writing, an Internet search on the phrase "strategic planning" yields

110,000,000 hits in just 0.42 seconds. Clicking deeper, one finds all manner of strategic frameworks and elements within those frameworks that companies could and should consider to create a complete strategy. These include, but are not limited to:

- Vision and Mission

- Identity and Values

- Operating Principles

- Corporate Strategy

- Market Strategy

- Product Strategy

- Technology Strategy

- Concept of Operations

- Management Plan

- Strategic Objectives

- Long-Term and Short-Term Goals

- Key Performance Indicators (KPIs) and Measures (KPMs)

- And the list goes on . . .

This book assumes most organizations already have many of these items in place and, because of this, many will not be covered in detail in this book. Instead, the focus is on those elements that are most relevant to success using the SOS2ROI approach. Vision, long-term goals, and the operating principles of the organization are examples of such critical elements.

Why Am I in This Line of Work?

While growing up in Colorado in the mid-1980s, I had a dream of going to the Air Force Academy and flying fighter planes, a la *Top Gun*.

Every chance I got, I went on tours of the Academy, drove around the public-access portions of the campus, and learned everything I could about attending one day. I even snagged a precious copy of the cadet handbook and started to memorize the code of conduct. I learned the minute features of historical airplanes so I could recognize them at a glance.

In short, I was a man with a plan.

Naturally, the application process required a comprehensive medical evaluation. I had no worries about this since I played multiple sports, was physically fit, had good eyesight, and did very well in school. I was a shoo-in, right? Yet, when the results came back, the vision section concluded:

"Candidate sees 20/20 but is not qualified for pilot training due to less than plano refractive error in any meridian."

Really? What's a plano? What's a meridian? *Noooooooooo*!

Now I'm no doctor, and I didn't know exactly what that meant. But what I did know was that for me, the likelihood of becoming a fighter pilot appeared (as far as I could "see") distant. What's worse, now the competition was tougher, because the Academy had most openings dedicated to future pilots. Furthermore, I resided adjacent to Colorado's Fifth Congressional District, which included the Air Force Academy, and was now competing with thousands of other candidates for precious few nonpilot openings and even fewer Congressional nominations. Despite having done well in school and sports, being considered an exceptionally well-rounded guy, and receiving great feedback from my admissions interviews, I didn't make it in.

I was devastated. I was sick.

But I swallowed my pride and did what I thought was the next best thing. I went to school on an ROTC scholarship and studied aerospace engineering. I figured if I couldn't go to the Academy and fly the jets in the sky, at least I could help design and build them on the ground.

When I graduated and entered the Air Force, I was assigned to my dream job: a program manager on the F-22 fighter jet. At the time, that plane was ending its preliminary design process and was the coolest. It was stealthy, sleek-looking, fast and furious.

As I moved from assignment to assignment, I became adept at quickly grasping the vast array of technologies on this and other airplanes, missiles, satellites, and collections of advanced technologies we can't talk about in this book. And one thing was certain: each came with its challenges, and the companies that build them did some amazing things even though the programs often cost a bit (or a lot) more and took longer than planned.

Through the years since the Air Force, and an executive and professional services career since business school, I have come to realize that I enjoy helping companies deal with complex and sophisticated technological and engineering challenges. I'm thankful to have been privy to many mistakes as well as some amazing successes. I have learned from hundreds of executives, and thousands of dedicated engineers, technicians, staff, suppliers, and customers. They have not only inspired me with their dedication and commitment to do the right things for their organization, but also to do the right things for purposes beyond themselves, like safety and freedom.

Even though I didn't get to fly as a fighter pilot for my career, I did finally get the opportunity to fly in a fighter jet as a result of winning a leadership award as a young captain. My reward was a day of training at Holloman Air Force Base in New Mexico, the site of Air Force fighter lead-in training. I experienced the High-G chamber, flew the simulators, and got a ninety-minute flight in a T-38 fighter trainer with heaps of loops, turns, and rolls, which left me thrilled, exhausted, and, not surprisingly, a bit sick. Par for the course, as it turns out.

It was cool.

Seeing Leaders on Their Best Day

Branching out on my own in mid-2005 was the best decision I ever made. I'm lucky that I get to wake up every day knowing that shortly, I will see my client on his best day ever.

> **They have not only inspired me with their dedication and commitment to do the right things for their organization, but also to do the right things for purposes beyond themselves, like safety and freedom.**

One such example was a group of twelve young engineers who were ridiculously smart and working to position their technology solution to many interrelated government customers. They were bright, but not yet seasoned, and we worked with them to help them understand how to frame strategic and operational benefits to solve real-world problems based on their technology, as well as how to speak and relate to economic, technical, and executive buyers. Long story short, we hosted a two-day event that was a massive success—so much so that many oft-critical customers said, "This is the best meeting this customer group has ever had." And a senior client, one of the most demanding and difficult chief engineers, said to me, "Wow, you guys have the best stuff I've ever seen."

Encouraging? Indeed.

But the topper was the pride radiating from those twelve engineers and their bosses. It was the stuff of legends. They had a real swagger in their step and were grinning ear-to-ear. They realized they had accomplished something amazing for the nation and for themselves. It's a moment that will serve as a waypoint for their entire professional life.

I loved that day.

Thankfully, there have been many such days. For the past decade, we've been blessed with the opportunity to help clients take on an array of diverse challenges. Some include:

- Rescuing programs, companies, and even nonprofit organizations from the brink

- Extending lean manufacturing principles into the more mysterious worlds of engineering design and strategic business change

- Creating contingency plans and mobilizing cross-functional organizations facing massive uncertainty

- Helping to solve the government agency challenges through innovative partnering and technology

They had a real swagger in their step and were grinning ear-to-ear.

- Transforming stagnant, swamp-like organizations nearing death into vibrant, flowing rivers of talent

- Enabling hyper-growth startups to surf the market wave to expand rapidly nationwide and even worldwide

It has been, and continues to be, a great pleasure to do what we do.

Why Write This Book? Why Read This Book?

Along the way, we've identified patterns of mistakes that clients make, and this book is an attempt to share some of our lessons.

It is our sincerest hope that you can apply some of these ideas and not only make your business system better today, but also build it stronger and more adaptable for the long haul ahead.

Many of the lessons are practical and are action-oriented. Before going into the practical, however, let's spend some time discussing the mindsets and attitudes critical for success; the *madness behind the method*. That is the subject of chapter three.

Chapter 2 Complexity Conqueror's Tactics

- Create a means to perceive, prioritize, and manage change, both proactively and reactively. Begin to build this capability into your organization. Leaders facing complexity must become outstanding adapters.

- Prepare to learn the tactics and techniques not only to repair cracks in the business system but also enhance capabilities needed to be more competitive.

- Form a vision for the kind of culture that will succeed amidst complexity. Be sure this culture includes ways of creating openness in the organization and broadening alignment to support priorities.

CHAPTER 3

The Critical Mindsets

When battling the Complexity Monster, it's important to be aware of not only its physical tactics but also its mental tactics. Thus, preparing for battle requires both physical and mental preparation, lest the adversary gain a foothold in the conqueror's mind.

In Homer's *Odyssey*, Odysseus was returning from war with his men by ship and was warned to steer far clear of the island inhabited by creatures called Sirens. The danger, as the story goes, is that the Sirens' beautiful singing was so compelling it could lull men to crash on the island's jagged rocks or even set foot on the island where they would confront the evil creatures and meet certain death.

For self-protection, only two techniques were certain. A sailor could place beeswax in his ears or tie himself to the ship. In the case of Odysseus, he longed to hear the Sirens singing, but insisted that his men tie him to his own ship's mast and put beeswax in their own ears. As they passed the Sirens, Odysseus heard and was mesmerized by the beautiful voices; then, entranced, he demanded that his men untie him so he could go to the island. They (naturally) refused. After the ship was far beyond the echo of the singing, Odysseus finally came back to reality, relieved at having successfully conquered the challenge.

Ten Critical Mindsets

A well-prepared mind is less vulnerable to manipulation and can anticipate and overcome the knowable traps the monster puts in its path. Experience teaches that critical mindsets can be crucial to helping strategic change go smoothly without succumbing to the attractive, yet ultimately fleeting temptations such as oversimplifying a truly complex undertaking, battling unwinnable complexity, or ignoring valuable complexity.

Although it can be argued that additional mindsets apply (I agree), the following ten are the most critical.

1: Treat Management Attention as Valuable Currency

Sometimes described as management bandwidth or leadership bandwidth, attention must be considered as valuable a factor in business success as anything else, including dollars or time. Change requires focus and attention, and if management is spread too thin, the change initiative will go more slowly. In chapter 9, the *Now, Next, Monitor* process will be introduced as an option to help the organization combat this specific issue. It will help to limit the amount of "change WIP (work in progress)" in the system so that management can focus on a very few key changes and get them done quickly.

2: Pursue True Alignment

Like driving with the emergency brake on, a misaligned team also slows progress. Either due to an excess search for priority and direction or disagreement about the plan, lack of alignment is pure waste.

Warning: beware of false alignment. It is not rare to hear the following from executive clients: "We agree with each other way too quickly. Because everyone is so busy,

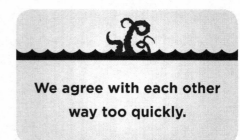

We agree with each other way too quickly.

and no one wants to make waves, our team rarely pushes back on the boss or with each other." This executive is calling himself and his peers on alignment that is not truly alignment after all. Knowing that this is the case is instructive, but what to do about it is the next mindset.

3: Invite Hard Conversations

Healthy teams encourage healthy debate and believe hard conversations should not only be accepted, but welcomed. Change is difficult work, and with such work comes conflict. As in any relationship, system, or organism, unresolved conflict festers and can become a huge issue over time. Yet with hard conversations, where conflict is resolved, one can find more alignment, better ideas, and greater commitment. Not every conversation needs to be a debate, but teams should not be afraid to take each other on, in the spirit of the mission, to forge the best possible solutions.

This isn't easy, however. For teams to get good at hard conversation requires a strong leader to facilitate them. Thankfully, many resources exist to build this skill. Strong leaders model this attitude and are open to tough conversations going both ways. When people fear their leaders, the leaders inevitably are not dealing with reality and solutions will be suboptimal (and the leaders will be the last to know).

4: Embrace Problems

Old problems that are continually repeated require a system fix at the root cause. Yet new problems are fuel for improvement because they reveal opportunities to make the system better. They also shed light on the Complexity Monster. Problems are the system telling you where it's aching and needs attention. Another way of thinking about it is, our goal is not to *avoid* problems but to solve them, so we get the chance to take on bigger ones.

Successful leaders view a problem like a newsflash announcing an opportunity to repair something in the system. Take advantage of these opportunities.

5: Work *On* the System, Not *In* the System

Especially in executive ranks, leaders must strive to invest as much time as possible working on improving the system, making it more productive, less error-prone, faster, and more valuable to customers. Working *in* the system is akin to playing Whac-A-Mole and, although it often provides temporary relief from aches and pains, rarely produces lasting change.

We often encourage leaders to think in terms of the *Colors of Leadership Time*:

- **Green Time**—time spent efficiently running the operational aspects of the business, solving new problems, and executing. This is how the business makes money day to day: hence, green time.

- **Red Time**—time spent fixing repeat issues, dealing with inefficient processes, attending excessive meetings, bad multitasking, and the incredible tragedy of rework: doing something over unnecessarily.

- **Blue Time**—time spent developing people and working to improve the business system. Blue time is the most valuable time. Developing people gives them more capacity, makes them more productive, and teaches them to solve issues correctly the first time instead of dealing with the same problems repeatedly.

Working on the business removes the inefficiencies in the business, eliminates the rework of the business, and optimizes necessary processes like scheduling and running meetings.

BLUE TIME	• Developing people • Repairing systems issues • Enhancing capacity and capabilities
GREEN TIME	• Running the day to day • Handling problems once • Managing normal operations
RED TIME	• Fire fighting • Fixing repeated problems • Inefficiencies and bad multitasking • Mistakes and rework

Leaders should strive to spend a majority of time in Blue.

6: Think Right to Left

Beginning where we want to end up and working backward from there helps get our minds out of the weeds and provides a clear, logical path that can be used to build the solution. Consider the perspective from the top of the mountain looking back down the hiked trail. Effective strategic workshops encourage teams to visualize standing at the summit, goals achieved, and then to think about what the path needs to be to have gotten there. It's that approach that helps elevate our thinking out of the current reality (weeds), and into the world of possibilities. It is often said, "Let's go from point *A* to point *B*." And while that often applies, sometimes teams need to simply abandon point *A* altogether and just build point *B* from scratch. This is an example of right-to-left thinking.

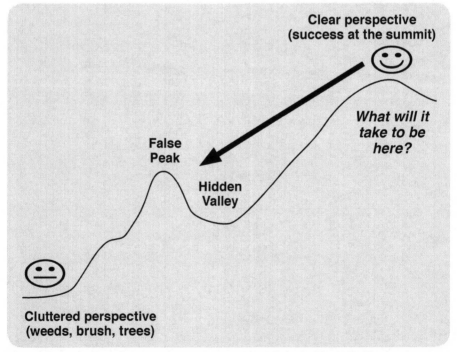

Creating a vision for success at the summit helps to clarify the journey required.

7: Jettison Bad Multitasking

Any multitasking that reduces either the quality or the speed of the highest-priority task is bad multitasking. Like texting while driving, watching the ballgame while on a date, or doing laundry while cooking risotto on the stove, bad multitasking is unwise, unsafe, and inefficient (typically resulting in a 30–70 percent productivity reduction in workshop exercises). It causes stress, yields more mistakes, and, per brain science, is literally impossible to do. According to Dr. Earl K. Miller, a neuroscientist at the Massachusetts Institute of Technology, "Don't try to multitask. It ruins productivity, causes mistakes, and impedes creative thought. Many of you are probably thinking, 'But I'm good at it!' Sadly, that's an illusion. As humans, we have a very limited capacity for simultaneous thought—we can only hold a little bit of information in mind at any single moment."

And that's just at the individual level. Think about how multitasking impacts entire teams and companies. The effects can be geometric in proportion. Experience shows that by holding a mindset hell-bent on getting rid of bad multitasking, organizations can begin to achieve an uncommon level of productivity. Several chapters in this book provide advice about how to remove bad multitasking from your portfolio of strategic change.

8: Experiment to Accelerate Learning

The improvement concept or idea and associated action plan will always be imperfect, but you can still act and plan to learn. Unfortunately, many leaders believe in a "one-size-fits-all" approach or a "build-it-and-they-will-come" approach. While those might work, and might even be necessary in limited situations, experimenting with a small implementation and then learning from the experience is the preferred way to go.

During an experiment (often called a pilot), learning can occur with minimum impact to the broader organization. Afterward, the approach can be adjusted and broadened out to full implementation. Change, especially amidst complexity, can often produce unintended consequences, and it's better to shake those out in advance than to find yourself in a crisis of failure and waste.

Perfecting a single-store concept before launching the national franchise, conducting focus groups for new products, and even introducing a new product in a limited geography are each examples of using experimentation to learn.

9: Mind the Risk

Many organizations are astute risk managers when it comes to day-to-day operational issues, major customer projects and programs, and functional processes like HR. At the same time, when planning major change initiatives, the same organizations simply ignore overwhelming evidence and consensus in academic and professional circles that typically 70 percent of change initiatives fail to achieve their objectives. If leadership decides not to manage that risk, the team is set up for failure. Just like any operational process, new product development, major project or plan, change initiatives should employ the fundamentals of risk management.

Risks that are common to change initiatives include but are not limited to:

- Lack of clarity of objective, value, or test of doneness

- Lack of stakeholder buy-in and resulting resistance
- Insufficient bandwidth of leadership or critical team members
- Lack of skilled personnel implementing the change
- Lack of priority in the organization

Consider these standard risks in addition to those that are known based on the nature of the project and the approach. Chapter 8 will explore ways to seek out mitigation steps and fold them back into plans to embed the fix and reduce the risk.

10: Engage Hearts and Minds

Change projects are inherently people-oriented. There are the planning team, the functional organizations, leadership, and often customers and suppliers to consider and engage. Most successful strategic changes can be traced back to a strong team that is fully engaged and committed to hitting the target. These change agents need to be able to build enough momentum to break through the corporate atmosphere and make a permanent mark on the organization.

As a leader, spending time with these teams is blue time of the highest order; however, not everyone is motivated the same way. One person may be motivated by achievement: "We are going to deliver more to customers." Another is motivated by competition: "We will crush our rivals." Still others may be motivated by the cause: "We are making the world a better and safer place."

It's critical to tap into what motivates and inspires the team, the stakeholders, and even the naysayers. Find out where the resistance is and inspire. Teach the team to do this as well. In this way, the leader is developing leaders and growing the organizational capability to manage change successfully. These are both major investments of bandwidth on the business system: blue time.

These critical mindsets provide a vital foundation for SOS2ROI. Encourage the team to embrace these, build the skills that underlie them, and watch your strategic initiatives flourish.

Chapter 3 Complexity Conqueror's Tactics:

- **Realize that success in strategic change goes beyond merely tools, processes, and frameworks. Mindset is critical.**

- **Understand the difference among green time, red time, and blue time. Strive to spend as much time as possible in the blue, and encourage team leaders to do the same.**

- **Plan to invest blue time to build your skills and that of your team to master the top mindsets. They don't come naturally or for free.**

- **Embrace the reality that to become great at change, the leader must become great at building a strong, open, and honest team that is not afraid to resolve issues, even if it's difficult or uncomfortable.**

- **Give yourself permission to be imperfect. Action accelerates learning, much faster than waiting.**

SECTION

Transforming from SOS to ROI

CONFRONT THE CHALLENGE

Face, contain, identify systemic "root causes"

While some monsters are not initially recognizable as such, there is always a moment where it is absolutely clear you are dealing with a real beast. It is at these revealing moments (SOS moments) where the leader faces the decision to confront the nemesis or instead take the easy route, delay acting, and hope the monster simply fades away. While in rare cases inaction can work, the vast experience is that most problems need to be confronted swiftly lest they fester and grow.

In the 1975 movie, *Jaws*, Larry Vaughn, mayor of a tourist-dependent beach community in New England, chose to ignore the monster. Despite multiple swimming deaths and expert evidence that a massive great white shark was responsible, he refused to confront the problem, fearing the loss in summer tourism income as a result of closing the beach. It wasn't until his own family was at risk that he finally relented and confronted the challenge.

Two Major Types of Problems

Every business faces an array of challenges every single day. And as noted American psychiatrist and author Theodore Rubin said, "The problem is not that there are problems. The problem is expecting otherwise and thinking that having problems is a problem."

OK, then. No problem.

Challenges (punctuated by SOS moments) tend to come in two flavors: system issues and unmet opportunities. This chapter discusses both and shows how others have confronted them head-on.

Robert in Crisis

The story of Robert illustrates a challenge that showed up as a systems issue.

Robert runs an electronics organization for a sophisticated manufacturer of high-tech products. A respected and loyal engineer, Robert rose steadily through the ranks and had assembled a great organization, with a lot of close confidantes and peers, covering two dozen specialized technical skills. His people were the best in the business, and Robert was doing well. Products were sophisticated, quality was high, and he had a great reputation inside the industry. One day, however, he was asked by his bosses what his succession plans were to replace these skills and hand off to the next generation. He hesitated, felt his heart racing, and soon called us in a panic.

After a short period, we discovered that of the twenty-four major skills in the organization, there was no succession plan for half, and that of his 800-plus engineers, a majority were eligible to retire in the next five years. Still panicking, but now armed with facts, Robert revealed that he had enjoyed the camaraderie of trusted peers and people he could count on near him. Yet, he realized that at the root of it all, he had created an organization that was less like a lake, with a free flow of talent in and out, and more like a stagnant bog. Long-term, he realized the need to transform his people-development approach to building a talent pipeline across all the major skill areas. Yet more critical, in the short term, he needed to quickly find a way to shore up the succession plans for a dozen critical-skilled areas (read, endangered species) before he and his parent company lost those skills forever.

In terms of assets, he had many senior experts, and he had a fresh crew of less-experienced, yet smart, motivated up-and-comers. In terms of liabilities, he had only a few senior managers and technical experts in the middle, and his products allowed no room for mistakes. Somehow, he needed not only to get the younger group up to speed quickly but also to extract the wisdom of the senior group as soon as possible.

Over the next several months, by implementing a cross-training program, identifying high-potential candidates, developing mentoring relationships, formal knowledge-transfer forums, investing in formal training, and identifying new opportunities to showcase leadership skills, Robert was able not only to significantly reduce the risk of the twelve skill areas, but also to grow his business. His organization won key contracts (one valued at more than $50 million), and was on track to turn his business from bog to lake.

The lesson? Just because you are healthy today doesn't mean you will always be healthy. Regular renewal must be part of an enduring organization.

In Robert's case, the lack of regular renewal in his talent pool ended up creating a problem that risked his entire organization; a true systems issue.

By contrast, the story of Wendy illustrates how her SOS moment showed up not as a systems issue, but as an unmet opportunity.

Wendy Facing Hyper-Growth

Wendy is a young, likable, ambitious entrepreneur who has an eye for market opportunity. Fiercely independent, she had been growing her kitchen equipment business steadily for just under a decade. When market trends began to favor her product, she began to get inquiries from the "big guys"—major distributors and retailers who could double or triple her business within a year. Yet, she had a challenge. She had limited capacity with her laborious, manual-intensive build processes and could safely increase capacity only through automation. In the months prior, sensing this, she and her team had tried to pursue automation without success; the business and technical ingredients for an automation solution remained a mystery. If she couldn't solve the mystery, she couldn't accept the new, lucrative, high-volume business, and those customers would look elsewhere.

It was a huge unmet opportunity, and she knew it.

Restless (her SOS moment), she asked us to help her search for clues and consider alternative approaches to get to a solution. After bringing in experts to analyze the problem and evaluate several technology alternatives, we found a partner who could bring together multiple proven inventions into a first-of-its-kind automation solution. Thus, Wendy could accept the larger business, deliver her product with greater than 90 percent on-time results (which she did), and grow her business nearly three-fold in a year (which she did) while setting the stage for what is now a literal global reach (which she has). Wendy's advice to other fast-growing entrepreneurs? "Your smarts will get you only so far, but your wisdom to also leverage the smarts of others can take you to the stratosphere."

In this case, Wendy had a good system. Her employees were well-trained, her customers were happy, and both her top line and bottom line were growing steadily. But her problem, her SOS, was an unmet opportunity for massive growth.

Whether the SOS is a symptom resembling a systems issue or a challenge to overcome an unmet opportunity, the situation is often a cry for help and demands immediate attention. The wise leader realizes that she needs to surround herself with smart people who can help expose the problem and accelerate the solution.

But the solution needs to be the right one. And that can come only from finding the real problem at its core.

Finding Root Causes

As a young Air Force officer, I was sent to the California Institute of Technology (Caltech) for an immersion in the art of statistical process control. The instructor, Alan Dunn, an expert in manufacturing and distribution and partner at what is now Capgemini consulting, told us the story of a large electronics assembly operation that was once thrust into chaos because the organization was having a difficult time keeping its inventory accurate.

But her problem, her SOS, was an unmet opportunity for massive growth.

As with most inventory systems, there were two ways to count. The first way was through the software database, which was updated when a supplied part arrived at the dock. In this case, the information was entered manually by a clerk. The second way was to conduct a physical inventory and count how many parts were on the shelf or in process. The problem was, consistently, the database and the shelf didn't match. For example, if the database said there were 100 dual-terminal capacitors, it was likely that the shelf only had ten.

Because the operation relied on accurate databases, when parts didn't show up for assembly because they were (surprisingly) out of stock, electronics couldn't be built and delivered to customers. Customers were upset, and management was stumped. Plant leadership had tried everything, and more than one manager had been fired for claiming, "Don't worry, I have it all under control." Yet the problem persisted. Frantic, management had spent countless hours, dollars, and developed many gray hairs guessing what was wrong. Yet it was only when another new plant manager, who had a sign above the entrance to his office that said, "Hope is not a fact," stepped back and logically searched for the root cause (using a variety of statistical techniques), that he ultimately discovered the department data entry clerk, Peggy, had dyslexia. For months, she had unknowingly transposed portions of the orders, created errors, and literally single-handedly brought the plant to its knees. As a solution, the department moved her to a different role, and the problem immediately went away.

Hope is not a fact.

As a leader, it is difficult to be more wasteful with time than fixing the same problem again and again with the wrong solution or, more often, an incomplete one. The first time it comes up, it's green time. Every other time? Red time.

Why do we do this? Because:

- We rationalize it's only a one-time thing, and that it will likely not come up again.

- We tell ourselves that the problem is real, but is likely to go away on its own.

- We justify that we have time only to triage, stabilize the situation with a Band-Aid or tourniquet, and get to the root cause later.

- We help the team solve a problem and assume that it's the correct solution without following up on either the accuracy of the solution or the implementation of the solution.

- We guess at the root cause, hoping that we got it right, but often don't go deep enough or broad enough.

Solving the mystery of root-cause is often hard work. Ever wonder why an episode of the television show *CSI* is an hour long and not less? The investigation takes time. The team needs to collect evidence, sort through clues, travel down dead-end paths, and expend a ton of physical and emotional energy. But what if the investigators could simply solve the case with their first guess? Then we could all move on to watching the next *Seinfeld* rerun, right? Even Albert Einstein may have had this in mind when he said, "If I had an hour to solve a problem, I'd spend fifty-five minutes defining the problem and five minutes thinking about a solution." As leaders, we know intrinsically it's better to solve the mystery than to act as if the mystery doesn't exist, or that

The investigation takes time. The team needs to collect evidence, sort through clues, travel down dead-end paths...

we've solved it without truly getting to the bottom of it. Yet, what are the true benefits of solving the root-cause mystery?

- By getting to the root cause, you can actually begin to solve the problem.

- By solving the problem right, you don't have to solve it again (in most cases).

- Gaining knowledge of areas that *aren't* the problem.

- The analysis can be depicted and explained to others. One can show the logical process and aid in stakeholder understanding and buy-in.

- You'll waste less time playing Whac-a-Mole (unless that's your thing).

- You'll spend less time in the red, and more time in the blue, improving other parts of the business system and developing your people.

Solve it once, solve it right, and it's gone forever.

A lot is written about the tools required to get to systemic root cause. Here is a summary of the most popular tools available for getting to root cause and taking corrective action.

A Refresher on Root Cause Tools

- **Brainstorming**. Often, the team knows more than we think they know. Listen to them. Take advantage of the combined experience of a diverse group and ask a focused question, such as:

  o "Why are we experiencing this issue?"

  o "What are other possible reasons?"

  o "What is the first thing we could do to correct the issue?"

- **Fishbone (Ishikawa) Diagram.** List possible categories of causes, and then potential likely causes within each category. From there, use a logical approach to eliminate possible causes and apply facts and information to focus the case on likely suspects.

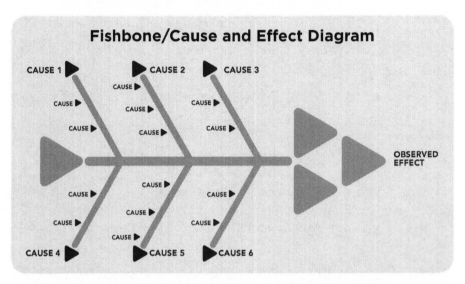

- **Five Whys.** Start with a symptom to a problem (like contamination in a product) and keep asking why did this happen. OK, but why did that happen? OK, but why did *that* happen? Repeating five times will likely find the root cause. This is partially how the manufacturing company in the example earlier found the dyslexic data entry clerk.

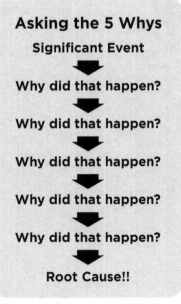

- **System Maps**. Model the chain of events—show the interactions, and how one element has an impact on the other. Show the iterative, often vicious, cycles. Once causes are identified, then solutions can be developed to reverse the vicious cycle. In one of our client engagements, a system map analysis revealed that the reason for consistently late deliveries was not the product build, but how accountability was allocated within the organization. Once that was addressed, the vicious cycle turned into a virtuous cycle, and on-time deliveries ensued, earning the company supplier-of-the-year honors from its largest customer.

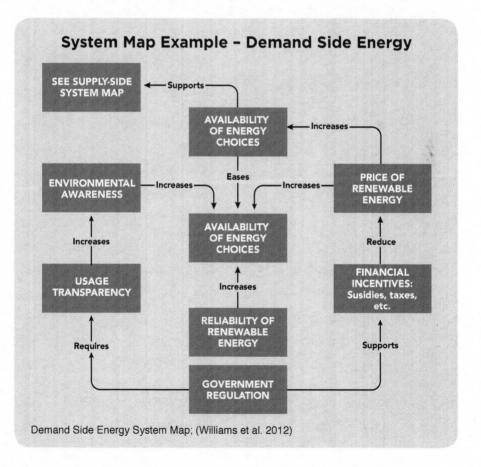

System Map Example - Demand Side Energy

Demand Side Energy System Map; (Williams et al. 2012)

- **Custom (or Combination) Assessments**. In complex organizations, many symptoms interact, and often a customized approach using a combination of the above tools is needed to reveal the most critical patterns and issues. Larger organizations get feedback from multiple sources (customers, government agencies, internal and external audits, employee surveys, consultants, and analysts). As it was for Anthony's team in chapter 1, the temptation is often for each department to react independently to each line-item in the litany of feedback, which often results in a rat's nest of overlapping and even competing actions. An integrated organic assessment is a great way to step back, hover above the complexity at 10,000 feet, and find the true patterns that reveal the root causes in the system.

A Word of Advice: Remember to Check the Soft Stuff

Many practitioners formally trained in root cause analysis and associated statistical tools will focus solely on logical and technical root causes. Yet many times, the driving forces of the system issues are broader. Often, they are about leadership, culture, and other nontechnical regimes that manifest themselves in day-to-day patterns of behavior. To get at these root causes, the analysis must consider those areas when searching for clues. By using a diverse team and seeking broad perspectives, there is an increased likelihood that the real issues will surface, even if the true root cause is you, the boss.

To summarize, these tools and a host of other proprietary tools developed by a litany of service providers (or "home-grown" within the company) should help indicate where the root causes lie. From there, formulate a solution.

But before any causes can be found, the challenge must be confronted, not avoided.

Once the team understands the root causes of one or even several problems, then the task of using those insights to improve the business system can be considered. That inside-out way of thinking about improvement is the subject of the next chapter.

Chapter 4 Complexity Conqueror's Tactics

- Take the attitude that problems are to be embraced and confronted. The complex business system is trying to communicate that something at the root needs to be addressed. Use it to gain insight and learn.

- After containing the initial circumstance, use a diverse and knowledgeable team to solve the mystery of root cause. A diverse team has multiple perspectives and can see a much more complete view than the boss alone.

- Once the root cause is identified, plan to solve it once, completely, and forever.

- Be sure to document the rationale and the logical investigation so that others can understand and buy into the solution. This also limits future undoing.

- Always allow interpersonal, cultural, communication-oriented, and other, softer areas of the operation to be clues in the investigation.

CHAPTER 5

REPAIR THE SYSTEM

Short-term fix, permanent fix, prevention

Many have described cancer as a monster.

In the Pulitzer Prize winning book, *The Emperor of All Maladies: A Biography of Cancer*, author Siddhartha Mukherjee describes cancer as "a monster more insatiable than the guillotine," and explains, "it is a disease of overproduction, of . . . unstoppable growth, tipped into the abyss of no control . . . unable to quench its initial demand (to grow) and thus transformed into an indestructible, self-propelled automation."[6]

This is a stark reminder of the previous chapter which discussed how it is critical to face the problem, lest it has time to fester and get worse.

Yet, facing the problem once is not enough. The real challenge is to ensure the issue (disease) is fully and completely eradicated. The conqueror must keep at it.

---

[6] Mukherjee, Siddhartha. *The Emperor of All Maladies: A Biography of Cancer.* New York: Scribner, 2011, p. 38.

Mukherjee describes one researcher's discovery about his process: "If you started off with 100,000 leukemia cells in a mouse and administered a drug that killed 99 percent of those cells in a single round, then every round would kill cells in a fractional manner, resulting in fewer and fewer cells after every round of chemotherapy: 100,000 . . . 1,000 . . . 10 . . . and so forth, until the number finally fell to zero after four rounds. Killing leukemia was an iterative process, like halving a monster's body, then halving the half, and halving the remnant half."[7]

In other words, eradicating the problem requires tenacity, repetition, and persistence until the point where the disease has been completely removed.

The same is true of repairing the system. The goal is to make sure that the problem goes away not just once, but is unlikely ever to return.

System Repairs versus Enhanced Capabilities

The next two chapters are about identifying opportunities to improve the business from two main sources. The first, covered in this chapter, is opportunity arising from issues that come from a broken business system (like a flat tire) and the second, in chapter six, is from capability enhancements that must be put in place (like a turbocharger) to achieve future goals (like racing the car). While these can be the same in rare cases, each often requires a different set of logic. Initially, the focus is on identifying opportunities to fix a broken business system.

---

[7] Ibid., p. 143

Opportunity Source 1: Fixing a Broken Business System

During my college days in the late '80s, the aerospace industry was at a standstill. Thus, most of the internships for graduating seniors were unavailable, and the majority of my aerospace engineering class were forced to take summer internships in less traditional settings. In my case, I got a summer gig at one of the Procter & Gamble paper plants where the company produced, among other things, paper towels and toilet paper. Not exactly rockets, stealth aircraft, or missiles, but I figured it would do for the summer.

During one week, the plant's only, massive, and oft-finicky paper machine (with its roughly 100 perfectly balanced ingredients) was having issues, not producing paper to the quality standard, and had to be shut down. Plant management scrambled to analyze why this was occurring. Despite using all the right tools from the previous chapter, days went by and they still hadn't arrived at the root cause.

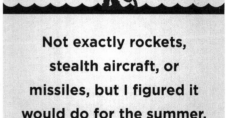

Not exactly rockets, stealth aircraft, or missiles, but I figured it would do for the summer.

Then one day, while the team experimented with some hunches, the paper machine started running perfectly again, literally out of the blue. One manager exclaimed, "Fabulous! Now we can get back to our normal jobs." But the plant manager, in his infinite wisdom, rebutted, "Listen, if we don't know the root cause of why it's better, then we also won't know why it will fail the next time."

A few short days later, they indeed found the root cause, implemented the fix, and the plant got back to normal operation.

In addition, they not only figured out the problem, but why it had happened in the first place, and implemented controls to prevent it in the future.

Sir Winston Churchill once said about problems, "A pessimist sees the difficulty in every opportunity; an optimist sees the opportunity in every difficulty."

The previous chapter discussed how to get to the root cause of a problem (whether an issue or an unmet opportunity) so you can solve the issue and move on with your day. That's a good use of green time. Problem solved, right?

> **Listen, if we don't know the root cause of why it's better, then we also won't know why it will fail the next time."**

But wait. Some questions:

- Why did the problem occur in the first place?
- How do you know the problem will not rear its ugly head again?
- What allowed it to happen?
- Will it occur again?
- How do we know?

To answer these questions, step back and make a couple of observations.

Observation: Organizations Are Systems

As with a mobile hanging from the ceiling, manipulating one element often can have an impact on all other elements.

The same is true of a business system.

Invented as a concept by McKinsey & Company in the early '80s, and expanded upon by Michael Porter at Harvard Business School, a business system is *a methodical procedure or process that is used as a delivery mechanism for providing specific goods or services to customers.*

Inherent in a business system are both the notion that several pieces make it up, and also the idea that many, if not all, of these pieces are interconnected. When solving a root cause, the context must be in terms of the entire business system. As discussed in chapter 1, business systems are getting more complicated and often more complex. No longer can they be modeled easily with predictable high-confidence results. Indeed, the Complexity Monster is having its way and must be dealt with.

So instead of merely asking, "What made this problem/ root cause occur?" ask, "What about the business system allowed it to occur?"

To illustrate, in the case of the dyslexic data entry clerk (see chapter 4), one could surmise that what was missing in the system was a set of formal job qualifications or employee screening tests to ensure that this, and perhaps other conditions, were not present in the employee candidate for that position.

So, in addition to solving the root cause (moving her to another position in the company), the organization had the chance to improve the system so that these types of issues didn't happen in the future. In a similar situation, this could be the responsibility of the HR function and the management of the shipping department. Who knows? Perhaps the same woman could create the new interview screening process to include a check for dyslexia.

- **Observation: Leadership Should Strive to Improve the System Continually**

In today's fast-changing, ever-competitive environment, mere survival often means continually improving the organization and the business system. For example, just because a firm can command high prices and market share today, doesn't mean it always will. Most likely, it will need to continue to reduce costs or enhance products (or both) to maintain margins for the long haul as new competitors encroach. This is true in nearly every type of organization or corporate function.

Thus, in all organizations, management has the obligation and necessity to continually improve the business system, making it more efficient, effective, and valuable to stakeholders. If not, the organization, failing to race upward to counteract the motion of a down-going escalator, might end up on the ground floor. And no stakeholder likes being on that floor. As an example, recall the organization that had created bog-like conditions by failing to renew their talent and workforce regularly. Thankfully, the organization was saved from the brink of collapse, but it took some serious triage and speedy rectification on the ground floor to make it happen.

The implication of these two observations is simple.

Whenever there is a problem, management should continually do all it can not only to identify the root cause of the problem but also to fix the business system so that the situation is unlikely ever to repeat.

If not, the organization, failing to race upward to counteract the motion of a down-going escalator, might end up on the ground floor.

A Primer on Fixing Broken Business Systems

Before diving deeper into our discussion of fixing broken systems, some definitions are in order:

- **Issue or Symptom**: Sign indicating the existence of a known problem or an unmet opportunity

- **Root Cause**: The initiating reason producing the issue or symptom, and likely the spot where intervention might compel a change. This is often a mystery.

- **Containment**: Action to limit or control damage (such as a product recall). This is often done before or in parallel with other actions.

- **Short-term Fix**: The immediate action, directed at the root cause (most often) to solve the issue and relieve the symptoms. This tends to be temporary.

- **System Gap**: The specific deficiency in the business system that allowed the root cause to occur in the first place.

- **System Improvement (or Repair)**: The approach, process, or method implemented to fix the system gap, so the problem is unlikely ever to occur in the future.

Returning to the assembly plant (from chapter 4) with an inventory problem, the *issue* was missed deliveries of electronic assemblies due to bad data in the inventory database. The *root cause* was that the clerk, Peggy, had dyslexia and was unknowingly entering bad data into the database. The *containment* was that all recent inventory that Peggy had entered during the previous period was deemed suspicious until it could be double-checked. The *short-term fix* was moving Peggy out of a data-entry role. The *system gap* was that dyslexia was incompatible with the clerk's original role, and there was no screening process in place to ensure it was caught. Finally, the *system improvement* was to ensure the hiring process for that position included a screen for dyslexia.

System improvements come from system gaps, which come from systems issues. At any one time, most organizations face multiple issues, with more than one root-cause mystery needing to be solved.

Examples of systems issues include:

- Quality control

- Delivery problems

- Process inefficiencies

- Employee confusion

- Miscommunication

- Customer complaints

- Repeated problems

- Supply-chain issues

- Employee turnover

- Mistakes and rework

- More

Choosing Which System Improvements to Work On

If the organization can solve each problem as it occurs, great. But often, leaders are so busy that many do not get past the short-term fix and containment phase, and the root cause is *never* addressed. The advice in these cases is to pick one issue at a time and go all-in until the system issue is addressed in such a way that it is virtually impossible for the problem to occur again. How do you know which to focus on?

- Identify at the top level what the system gap is, including a brief description of what the system improvement might look like.

- For each system improvement, ask, "What is the value of fixing this?"

- Rank-order the improvement opportunities in terms of value (e.g., financial, strategic, cultural).

- When you are ready to implement, complete the highest-value items first.

- Begin by focusing on one item only and get it accomplished.

Then work on the next one. Don't attempt too many at once, lest you become overwhelmed and consumed by too much WIP (work in process). Invariably, productivity will plummet, and you will more than likely be content with containment and rationalize it with hope.

- At the end of the day, if the priority is unclear, just start with one of the improvements; waiting or multitasking is worse than picking the wrong exact priority.

Section III will focus more on how to manage a portfolio of improvement initiatives. Suffice it to say for now that it is far better to focus on one thing and go all the way to fixing the root cause and system gap than trying to make multiple improvements. Like a bridge over a treacherous canyon, half a solution isn't.

> **Don't attempt too many at once, lest you become overwhelmed and consumed.**

Technology-Oriented System Repairs—a Spacecraft Example

Here is a common example (experienced in one form or another by every company ever to launch a spacecraft) of a spacecraft deployment gone awry. The story goes like this:

When a spacecraft is launched, it is always in a compressed, or "stowed," configuration. The antennas, the sensors, the solar panels and other devices are scrunched up and folded together so that the craft will fit into the top of the rocket.

Once in space, however, the spacecraft begins a series of delicate movements called "deployments," in which the stowed configuration opens and becomes the operational configuration. The solar panels are expanded and pointed at the sun to bring energy to the spacecraft and recharge the batteries. The antennas are unfolded and pointed to the ground or to another satellite. The sensors are moved into position and pointed at their intended target for their mission. Critical to this operation are both the sequence and timing of these events. If the parts don't transform from stowed to operational configuration in the exact right sequence and timing, there is a risk for very bad things to occur, which all spacecraft companies have experienced at one time or another.

In many of these retellings, a satellite was launched perfectly, then began its transformation from stowed to operational configuration as planned. But then something odd occurred. Like two cars facing each other in a narrow alley, two of the components blocked each other and forced a standstill. In one commercial-satellite case, the hindered component was the antenna, which communicated vital status information and also received commands from the ground. It was blocked; therefore, mission control (e.g., Houston) couldn't get a signal regarding what was wrong or tell the spacecraft how to fix itself.

Back on Earth, panic ensued. There was no way of knowing if the solar panels were deployed correctly, the status of the battery, or how much energy and time they had left. Assuming the worst-case scenario (a couple days of battery power without recharging), the team worked around the clock to find a way to communicate with the satellite, learn what was going on, and identify a fix to allow it to continue its deployment into its operational configuration. In the end, after several creative maneuvers, the team ultimately saved the spacecraft.

Like two cars facing each other on a narrow alley, two of the components blocked each other and forced a standstill.

After a thorough root-cause analysis, it was determined that during testing in the factory prior to launch, a mechanical part had been replaced with a new part to enable the spacecraft to pass a test; not a big deal in and of itself. But no one realized that the new part had physical characteristics that could cause mechanical interference. And because it was not documented as a change, the engineers had never had a chance to see or evaluate the new part to reexamine the deployment sequence and assess the risk of interference.

The root cause of the issue was clearly a mechanical part with different dimensions than the original. Yet the system gap turned out to be a lack of documentation and configuration management. In this case, the system improvement was to beef up the configuration management disciplines during testing, including training the team to ensure that nearly all changes to spacecraft configuration, regardless of how slight, are documented and implications analyzed by the engineers prior to launching.

For spacecraft companies, these prove to be tough but valuable lessons. Yet they also enable huge improvements to the business system and prevent future mistakes, thus saving many millions of dollars, if not more.

Nontechnical System Repairs—a Leadership Example

Another example deals with a less technical system gap around organization.

Gary is an engineer, manufacturing industry veteran, and gritty president of an electronics component supplier. His organization was facing higher demand than normal and was delivering late to his largest, and very upset, customer, who was threatening to go elsewhere soon. On a quest to succeed, Gary asked us to dig deeper, facilitate a series of strategic workshops, and help to find the root cause and identify the system improvement.

After interviewing the teams, it became apparent the root cause was that production priorities were being set by both department managers and functional managers, and often conflicted. Not wanting to upset either boss, the delivery teams were doing their best to accommodate both sets of requests but were forced to compromise daily. This had the result of decreasing the delivery rate for the most important parts. Because of our engagement, Gary realized that he also had a systems gap: his organization was set up without clear lines of authority, and decision processes were convoluted and inconsistent. By organizing his division by product lines with clear lines of authority, including the level of decision-making, he ultimately helped immediately ramp up the rate of dedicated deliveries to customers.

As a result, his deliveries caught up within three months, and the division won supplier-of-the-year from their largest, and previously most frustrated, customer. Gary's moral? Many times, performance issues aren't about performance; they are truly about people, leadership, and communication. "It's the job of the leader to fix the system," he said.

Of the two major types of improvements, system repairs are about making current business systems better. However, in today's changing, highly competitive environment, the stakes continue to be raised, and new capabilities must be

Many times, performance issues aren't about performance; they are truly about people, leadership, and communication.

created. To be successful, companies need to be habitually on the lookout for opportunities to enhance existing capabilities and even build new ones. This is the subject of chapter 6.

Chapter 5 Complexity Conqueror's Tactics:

- Take a deep breath and embrace your responsibility to continuously improve the business system that you lead.

- Cultivate a mindset and culture that embraces issues and sees them both as sources of rare insight into your business system and as opportunities to improve.

- Understand the difference between the root cause of an issue and the system gap that caused it; solve both.

- With multiple issues, identify the one or very few that are the highest value to solve first and then solve them. Don't let up; continue until it becomes unlikely that the issue will ever occur in the future.

- Consider that most organizations realistically have the bandwidth to repair only one or two high-impact systems issues at a time.

BUILD CAPABILITIES

High-impact enhancements - adapt & compete

Although the Complexity Monster can be aptly compared to historical and mythological creatures, or even disease, it can also be shown to have similarities to villains in popular culture.

For instance, the Complexity Monster can often slow down an organization like the *Batman* villain, Mr. Freeze. After a terrible accident, Mr. Freeze survives via a refrigeration suit and uses his freeze gun to immobilize everything and everyone in his path. His victims, once attacked, remain motionless, unable to move as they become, literally, frozen in time.

In business, it is easy to get overwhelmed by the complications of daily activity—fighting fires, reacting to problems, and laboring to contain and repair system leaks. In this mode, it is easy to become self-absorbed and internally focused, tempted to ignore or minimize the importance of changes in the external environment. Complexity conquerors, aware of internal challenges, must avoid the freeze gun and regularly gauge external factors to identify what enhanced capability solutions (products, services, efficiencies, etc.) might be offered to meet the evolving needs of the marketplace.

Needs Often Arise from Necessity

Over the past decade, the United States prison system has been facing a growing and alarming challenge. Inmates have been using cell phones from inside prisons to perpetrate crime on the outside. At one point, according to inmates, the black-market prison price for a contraband cell phone was upwards of $1,500.[8]

But wait: are cell phones allowed in prisons? No. Are there rigorous screening and inspection protocols in place to prevent cell phones, chargers, and other electronic devices from entering the facilities? Of course there are. Well, then how is this happening? The answer: some lower-paid staff, vulnerable to bribes, have been enlisted to help the inmates, and the inmates have also used an array of amazingly creative means to get cell phones into the facility.

In one notable case, a basketball that looks much like the standard-issue version from the prison yard, was thrown over a fence, and sewn inside were dozens of small cell phones and chargers that were then simply picked up and walked into the facility. Someone was making money hand-over-fist.

Both public and private prisons have attempted to fix the system to ensure it could never happen again, but the challenge is difficult and some progressive states realized they needed to think differently. They realized they needed to build a new capability to combat this problem.

---

[8] http://www.gorillaconvict.com/2012/04/cell-phones-in-prison/, accessed 4/7/17

Working with the cellular carriers, and some sophisticated technology from a client of ours, states began to prototype a solution that (legally) rendered contraband cell phones useless inside the prison. The logic? Once the device is useless (e.g., it doesn't connect to the cellular network), then the demand goes away. Problem solved.

Many states are prototyping this capability and making plans to roll it out into multiple prison facilities.

The lesson? Sometimes, issues can't be solved with only a system repair. In these cases, enhancing the capabilities of the organization and innovating might be required.

Opportunity Source 2: Enhancing Capabilities to Compete at the Next Level

Thus far, the focus has been about creating solutions to improve (repair) the business system.

Imagine, however, that an organization finds and solves each of its system gaps and has a theoretically perfect system with no issues. Is that enough? Not necessarily. Better than a perfect system, it needs to be the *right* system with the right capabilities operating at the right speed. The organization needs a system that can respond to the demands of the external business environment (e.g., customers, suppliers, and competitors). Organizations need to always be on the lookout for capability enhancements to ensure they not only fix the current business system but also are building the future business system in relation to their goals.

But before you can build capabilities the right way, you need to know where you want to go.

Using the automobile analogy, the car has fixed its root cause of having a flat tire, putting air in the tires or installing run-flat tires to avoid a future puncture. At this point, the car is running well. Is that enough? Well, if the goal is shopping, then OK. But if the goal is racing, then perhaps a capability enhancement like a turbocharger is in order.

Capability Enhancements Derive from Goals

There are countless books on goal-setting, and this book will not cover all the ways to state goals except to suggest the following as a foundation for identifying capability enhancements:

- Goals should be long-term in nature, three to five years out.

- There should be few goals (no more than five to eight).

- The goals should include a mix of financial (like gross margins or cash flow), operational (like inventory turns or on-time performance), and people-oriented (like retention rate or employee satisfaction).

- They should be SMART[9] (Specific, Measurable, Achievable, Relevant, and Time-based), so it is clear when they are met.

Typical goals are often set in the context of the following:

- Sales and revenue, including growth

- Profit margins

- Cash flow

---

[9] Note: The SMART acronym was first defined in Dolan, George T., Arthur Miller, and James Cunningham. "There's a S.M.A.R.T Way to Write Management Goals and Objectives." *Management Review* 70, no. 11 (November 1981): 35.

- Market positioning and share
- Customer satisfaction
- Operational goals (such as productivity)
- Employee turnover/ satisfaction
- Shareholder value
- More

If the goal is racing, then perhaps a capability enhancement like a turbocharger is in order.

While system improvements deal with solving systems issues, capability enhancements are those improvements in which a new capability is created for the organization that did not previously exist. Often, this is a stretch that allows the organization to expand in a given area. New capabilities, once stable and mature, eventually become another part of the core business system.

Examples of capability enhancements include but are not limited to:

- Geographic expansion
- Technology implementation
- Automation systems implementation
- New products or services
- New processes
- Industry certifications
- Mergers and acquisitions
- Partnerships

- Strategic hires
- More

How to Identify Capability Enhancements

Capability enhancements are identified both in the context of goals and in the context of the environment in which the organization is operating. This includes the regulatory environment, the buying behavior of customers and consumers, competitive behavior, the cycle of the industry, how much innovation is occurring, etc. As such, one capability that should be in place in every organization is the ability to regularly assess the external environment to identify trends, dynamics, and patterns. If neglected, the organization could find itself in a plight similar to the lowly aircraft technicians in the movie, *Fletch*. In one popular scene, Fletch (impersonating an industry expert) lambasts the naïve mechanics for not keeping up with industry trends, exclaiming, "Come on guys, it's so simple, maybe you need a refresher course! It's all ball bearings nowadays!"

Some organizations keep this analysis and planning function in-house, while others rely on trusted third-party advisers to work in concert with the organization to understand the business environment.

Once goals are in place and the business environment is understood, the killer

One capability that should be in place in every organization is the ability to regularly assess the external environment to identify trends, dynamics, and patterns.

capability-enhancing question is, "Given our goals and the market/ competitive/business environment, what must we become in order to credibly succeed?"

EXAMPLE: FOOD PACKAGING CAPABILITY ENHANCEMENT (INDUSTRY CERTIFICATION)

One of our clients serving the food industry established a growth goal that could be met only by targeting increasingly sophisticated retailers that demanded only the highest food safety standards. The company determined that in order to credibly compete with the big guys, they needed to enhance their capabilities to become a certified food-safe supplier. This included:

- A certified food-safe portfolio of products

- A certified food-safe process to manufacture those products

Thus, they created an initiative that went something like the following:

> **Title:** Become a Food-Safe Supplier

> **Description**: Formally certify existing and all new products and processes to independent, respected, third-party food-safety standards

Over several months, as the company began to complete this initiative, additional opportunities arose to compete for larger accounts. Working tirelessly, yet in a focused manner, the company installed enhanced capabilities and successfully passed the third-party audits. After certification was complete, some big accounts, satisfied with the food-safety standards of the vendor, placed significant orders. As with many new capabilities, the organization had to develop new processes or mature existing ones to create something it didn't have before.

> Like briefly flicking on the light in a dark room, rare events provide valuable insight into the business system and provide fleeting but valuable moments of clarity.

ADAPTABILITY: THE MUST-HAVE CAPABILITY ENHANCEMENT

Today, as businesses are becoming more complicated and complex, it is often difficult to see the entire system at once, much less predict how it will operate or which initiatives will produce the intended results. That means organizations need to become increasingly more adaptable, both to the behavior of their business system and to the changing environment in which they operate. One way to build adaptability is to respond to events. Even if these events are difficult, such as issues or rare SOS moments, they provide a valuable function. Like briefly flicking on the light in a dark room, rare events provide valuable insight into the business system and provide fleeting but valuable moments of clarity. Learning to seek out and respond to these issues more often, more quickly, and more naturally will build increasing adaptability into your organization.

Chapter 6 Complexity Conqueror's Tactics

- Ensure that the organization defines a small set of clear and measurable long-term goals from which to derive capabilities.

- Consider your capability to analyze and understand the business and market environment and adapt on a regular basis.

- Use established goals and the environmental reality to drive opportunities for building enhanced capabilities that support both maintaining the current level of performance and competing at the next level.

- Resist the temptation to *always* start building capabilities from where you are today; sometimes, a teardown and new build are better than a remodel.

CHAPTER 7

> # BROADEN ALIGNMENT
> ## Diverse stakeholder vantage points, priorities

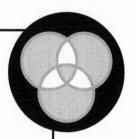

Even perfect ideas will not succeed without people on board, literally as well as figuratively.

Mutiny on the Bounty, a 1932 novel by Charles Nordhoff and James Norman Hall that has been made into several films, tells the story of the 1789 real-life mutiny aboard HMS *Bounty*, led by master's mate Fletcher Christian against the ship's captain, William Bligh, during the vessel's expedition to Tahiti.

As the story goes, at some point, camaraderie between Bligh and his crew worsened after he began handing out increasingly punitive penalties, blame, and cruelty. It is said Christian received a disproportionally high share.

The films assert the common view of Bligh as an overbearing monster and Christian as an unfortunate victim of the journey's odd events. Yet, more recently, not everyone shares these views.

In fact, more modern historians contributed to a more benevolent understanding of Bligh.

One such historian, John Beaglehole, described Bligh as a progressive and rational naval officer with one major flaw: "[Bligh made] dogmatic judgments which he felt himself entitled to make; he saw fools about him too easily . . . thin-skinned vanity was his curse through life . . . [Bligh] never learnt that you do not make friends of men by insulting them."[10]

Regardless of one's view on Bligh (a monster or a leader who did not suffer fools kindly), at the end of the day, the mutiny occurred on his watch, and that is precisely what the complexity conqueror seeks to avoid as he sets on the journey of transformation. Instead of pitting your team against you, seek to broaden alignment so that the (already difficult) change journey profits as the entire crew paddles in the same direction.

The People Side of Transformation

In the previous two chapters, we defined improvement opportunities as those system improvements and capability enhancements that, if implemented, will have a dramatic impact on achieving goals. But before flying headlong into action planning, leaders and key stakeholders need to get aligned around the vision and the priorities. In short, it's time to talk about people.

As chapter two mentions, this book will focus more of its attention on those elements of strategic planning most relevant to the success of the SOS2ROI approach. Indeed, not every tool, framework or possibility will be covered

---

[10] Beaglehold, James C. *The Life of Captain James Cook*: Stanford, Stanford University Press, 1974, page 498.

This chapter starts with vision and team alignment, then discusses the role of leadership off-sites as an accelerant, and ends with a brief discussion about setting priorities.

Setting Vision

"If one does not know to which port one is sailing, no wind is favorable."
—SENECA THE YOUNGER, ROME , FIRST CENTURY AD

Think about vision as the summit of a mountain. At the top, the journey is complete, and you've arrived at your destination. You've been through the ups and the downs, the switchbacks, the stream crossings, the false peaks, the plateaus, the meadows, and are now above tree-line and taking it all in: the vistas, the crisp air, the breeze, and the rich sense of accomplishment.

A good question for teams is, "Imagine you are on the mountaintop, journey complete; what do you see?" Their answer provides clues to their vision.

A good vision will have the following characteristics:

- A significant distance into the future (enough to be credible; perhaps five to ten years, but some effective visions are longer and, increasingly more lately, are shorter).

- Holistic: the vision needs to encompass the entire business system. This allows everybody in the organization to see themselves in the vision.

- Specific: one should be able to describe this vision with specific adjectives, attributes, features, and elements. It should have color, texture, smell, emotion, and life. For example, the home security firm, ADT, once had a vision depicted by a very simple image. The image was a blue ADT sign stuck in the snow in front of an igloo with the phrase, "Until the last house is secure." That is specific.

- Inspiring: it should motivate action and be compelling to the organization so that everyone is motivated to go above and beyond the call of duty.

- Challenging: the vision should stretch the organization. An inspiring future often will be difficult to achieve, but worth it. A lackluster vision or one that is easy to achieve isn't very inspiring.

With a solid vision, the organization can move to enhance the capability required to make it a reality. Each move can be (ideally) placed within the context of the vision itself. With this relationship in place, the leader can provide logic and rationale behind "why we are doing what we are doing," even though it may be difficult or unpopular. Explaining the logic and rationale is a great way to inspire the troops and get them marching in the right direction.

You've been through the ups and the downs, the switchbacks, the stream crossings, the false peaks, the plateaus, the meadows, and are now above tree-line and taking it all in.

The Importance of Alignment

Experience argues that alignment is critical to success. If the team, as well as key stakeholders, are not aligned to the vision and to implementing improvement opportunities, then they will be less committed to success and not give their all. This is especially true when some in the organization feel threatened or otherwise uneasy about the impending change, and fervently resist. In this case, when challenges emerge, the impetus will not be there to overcome those challenges, and the plan is certain to fail in terms of its potential results. Alignment is an absolute necessity, especially around the following three areas:

- the vision, ideas, and priorities of the transformation

- the specific action plans and investments of time, dollars, and bandwidth

- the team itself; what it needs to be as a team to ensure success

And while the first two areas will be explored throughout the remainder of this book, the question of the team is addressed below.

Four Questions for Strong Teams

Dr. Robert Clark, professor of management at Loyola Marymount University (Los Angeles) and frequent collaborator with this book's author, encourages leaders to ask themselves and their teams four questions to gain clarity around strengthening how they should operate as a group. He suggests groups actually take the time to think hard about what it looks like to be a great team and then consider asking it this way.

To be successful to fulfill your mission and strategy:

1. Do you need to be a team?

2. If so, what kind of a team do you need to be?

3. What actions should we take to get there from where we are today?

4. What actions am I (personally) willing to take to make that a reality?

Expanding further:

1. DO YOU NEED TO BE A TEAM?

These days, the word "team" is thrown around like candy. Here, when referring to being a team, it means not just being *called* a team, but truly *acting* like a team, functioning as a team. Yet today, the question of whether you even need it is most often ignored. Patrick Lencioni, in his book, *Overcoming the Five Dysfunctions of a Team,*[11] states: "building an effective, cohesive team is extremely hard." The implication: make sure you want to be a team before you fly headlong into the endeavor.

But before moving too much further, consider what a well-functioning team indeed is. John R. Katzenbach and Douglas K. Smith, in their *Harvard Business Review* article, "The Discipline of Teams," provide a helpful definition:

"A team is a small number of people with complementary skills who are committed to a common purpose, set of performance goals, and approach for which they hold themselves mutually accountable."[12]

---

[11] Lencioni, Patrick. Overcoming *The Five Dysfunctions of a Team: A Field Guide*. San Francisco: Jossey-Bass, 2005.

[12] Katzenbach, John R., and Douglas K. Smith. "The Discipline of Teams." Harvard Business Review. August 25, 2015. Accessed January 04, 2017. https://hbr.org/2005/07/the-discipline-of-teams.

Must all groups of people be teams? No. Think about it this way. If the work is better done by individuals reporting to the boss and no internal collaboration is required, then you don't need to be a team. If the answer is "no," then you can stop the questioning and

Explaining the logic and rationale is a great way to inspire the troops and get them marching in the right direction.

move on to the next agenda item. Yet, given the interdependent nature of modern work, the answer will most likely be "yes." You will likely choose to be a team.

This may seem trivial, yet asking the question is important, because you get the individuals to make the decision they need to be a team, not just have some coach or consultant tell them, or worse just assume, they need to be a team.

2. IF SO, WHAT KIND OF A TEAM?

Once all are in agreement to be a team, the next question speaks to what type of a team. To illustrate, consider a sports team. Are you a track team, where everyone shows up to the track in the same uniform, does their own thing without much interaction, and the individual points are added up to form the team score? In the track team, the most interaction is in the 4×100-meter relay, where the runners must pass the baton, but beyond that, are pretty much on their own. It's more about being a member of the team and less about acting like a team.

Or on the opposite extreme, are you a basketball team? A basketball team is highly collaborative. Here, points are scored by individuals, but the team needs to call plays, set picks, pass, and be in the right spot on the court to put the scorer in position. On the basketball floor, everyone has a role, and, importantly, no one is alone.

Of course, in the middle are other sports, such as baseball. There is a team, but at times you are on your own (like batting solo), and other times you are in high collaboration (like base runners in a hit-and-run or a defensive six-four-three double-play).

Indeed, the sporting metaphors could go on and on, and others as well (orchestra versus solo, chef versus wait staff in a kitchen). The point, however, is to find a way to describe what kind of a team you need to be. A tip on what kind of a team: Focus on how it needs to score points. Making baskets to score points requires a much different kind of a team than simply adding up the scores of individual track efforts.

Another tip here is to go back to your vision and ask, "Given our vision, what type of a team must we become to achieve it?"

Think about what attributes the team would have if successful, how it would act, how it would make decisions, agree to treat one another, take initiative, and overall how it would it behave. Write those things down and evaluate any gaps, both big and small. Also, identify where the team is strong and are currently operating well.

As an example, one client had a team in which the leaders had all grown up in operations, solving issues and putting out fires daily. This same skill was needed to achieve the future vision as well, and this team was expert at reacting to problems and fixing them. What they lacked, however, was proactive scanning for opportunities. That was the gap, because they needed both to succeed.

3. WHAT ACTIONS SHOULD WE TAKE TO GET THERE FROM WHERE WE ARE TODAY?

Is there a gap between where the team is today and where it needs to go? Most often, if the vision is inspiring and challenging, then yes, a gap likely exists. And in terms of thinking about opportunities for improvement (as in chapter 6), building a better team is more like enhancing a capability than repairing the systems problem. So, then, the question "What actions should we take to get there from where we are today?" should consider the gaps and what is missing. Write these down as well.

A typical example is around communications. It is rare that a team will be operating with

A tip on what kind of a team: Focus on how it needs to score points.

perfect communications. Often—especially if there is a lack of clarity around vision, goals, plans, priorities, and how the team should function—there is a lot of confusion, and it manifests itself in poor communications. Things get missed, decision-making is unclear, and people's feelings get hurt.

By identifying the actions that can be taken by the team to fill the major gaps, they are well on their way. Good, yes, but not enough.

4. WHAT ACTIONS AM I (PERSONALLY) WILLING TO TAKE TO MAKE THAT A REALITY?

To get to the heart of building a strong team, relevant to how they score points, everyone must personally come to the table with a commitment. If the group agrees, "Yes, we need to communicate better," then each member needs to understand how he or she can communicate better. So, for each major gap, go all the way down to the individual level, and ask each member to make a personal commitment.

For example, if the group decides that a team gap is "We need to share information more freely," and team member Fred is the consummate example of the information hoarder, then Fred would need to be open to doing a better job of sharing information freely for the entire team to get the benefit. In addition, it would be up to the team to define what that might look like for Fred.

As a practical matter, groups often identify five to six things they believe are important to their team operation. These are often called operating principles. And for each one, there may be a set of related behaviors. For example, if a team decides a key operating principle is "respect for one another," then the behaviors associated with that might include showing up to meetings on time, active listening, and communicating in a respectful manner. Some teams build posters and plaques of both operating principles and behaviors, sign them, and place them prominently in the work area as a constant reminder.

In most cases, teams need to be stronger. This strength requires focused priorities, action, and individual commitment. Unfortunately, too often teambuilding is rah-rah and navel gazing, and isn't strategic whatsoever. Using a strategic process (such as the four questions above) to derive the nature of the team needed for success is a better way to go. And as the old Right

Guard commercial so eloquently stated, "Anything less would be uncivilized."

Strategic Off-site as an Accelerant

As discussed at the beginning of this section, SOS2ROI can be an iterative process. And while the steps do indeed have a logical flow, they might need to be repeated to arrive at an acceptable solution. While some steps might be handled by small teams working temporarily in isolation (identifying a root cause of a systems issue, perhaps), the alignment step does not work that way. Alignment is often a gritty back-and-forth process that requires dialog, discussion, and clear-headed thinking through the options and choices. Strategic off-sites (or retreats) function as a great way to have those kinds of interactions and quickly gain the required alignment to both the vision and the implementation plan.

With the right planning and execution, leadership off-sites can indeed serve as a powerful solution.

For your next off-site event, consider these five simple guidelines.

Step 1: Decide Where You're Headed

Off-sites should be viewed as accelerating events that propel you toward your objectives. Off-sites support end goals. Often teams say, "Hey, our last off-site was fun. The golf was great, but I can't remember what we accomplished." Think of an airport tram. It can get you to your terminal more quickly than walking, but you need to know your gate number beforehand so you board the right tram. An off-site can function in much the same way: decide and document your goals before getting started. With a strong directional sense and clear objectives, the off-site program will stay more focused and energize the team.

Step 2: Prepare

An off-site requires more preparation than a weekly staff meeting. This is an investment of time and money that can yield long-term results. Ideally, allow three to six weeks to plan the off-site, prepare the participants, get stakeholder insights, assemble and analyze supporting content, and distill findings into areas of potential action. A defense software group conducted two off-site pre-sessions—one a month prior, another a week prior—to refine the plan, answer clarifying questions, and build buy-in and appetite for their dynamic three-day event. This level of preparation ensured that the team was ready to go when they arrived.

Step 3: Modulate the Aperture of the Conversation

In a camera, the aperture controls the amount of light allowed into the system. In leadership, "wide aperture" equates to a brainstorming session that maximizes the speed and flow of new ideas and fully engages the team. On the other hand, a "narrow aperture" focuses the conversation on setting specific goals, milestones, or making decisions. In designing the off-site, decide which segments or modules should be wide-aperture and which should be narrow, so that each conversation delivers the optimal results and team buy-in. Selecting and adjusting the aperture of the conversation is a best practice that pays high dividends in results.

Step 4: Focus! Less is More

Most off-sites are a buffet of "wish we could bring it up in staff meeting" topics, leading to too much content, too many objectives, and not enough time to discuss and develop the most important priorities. Resist this temptation. Instead, clarify a small set of critical objectives for the event—for example, one for the team, one for strategy, and one for the execution plan. The most successful teams have even created an off-site vision (a clear, concise statement of intent) to keep participants aligned before and during the event.

Step 5: Build in Implementation

How many times have you been to a high-energy off-site, only to lose all that momentum when you returned to the office? Implementation often falters because off-site promises are overcome by the "tyranny of the urgent," from catch-up email to the storm of daily activity. Instead, have a clear action plan built in to the off-site and start implementing before the off-site ends, so the team leaves with immediate progress and a plan to continue.

Small actions such as scheduling a follow-up meeting, complete with a room assignment, agenda, dial-in number, etc., helps immensely. As a critical part of establishing strategic priorities, be sure to create a "stop-list" of tasks and projects seen as no longer critical or those which can be delayed for a set time, to make room for the new areas of focus generated at the off-site (more about this in chapter 12). Schedule regular follow-up meetings with the leadership team and revisit strategy on a regular basis. This will unleash the power of the team, build confidence and focus, and accelerate the organization toward achieving planned results.

With an off-site retreat set up for success, you can focus on getting the most out of the event. And often, one of the important conversations leaders have is around setting priorities.

Setting Priorities

Not all opportunities for improvement are created equal. Even if they were, it's not possible to do them all

"Hey, our last off-site was fun. The golf was great, but I can't remember what we accomplished."

anyway. So, priorities must be established.

There are various methods one can use to set priorities, and one size doesn't fit all. Here are some important guidelines:

- Involve the group in the priority-setting process. This ensures everyone has a chance to weigh in on what they think the priorities might be and why. Even if the final decision is not the one they originally proposed, their involvement is more likely to engender commitment in the end.

- Combine like opportunities where possible. Choosing from a list of twelve is much easier than trying to choose from a list of twenty that is really a list of twelve.

- Ask focusing questions such as, "Where should we place our bets?" This ensures the group is thinking about how to allocate scarce resources (labor, dollars, time, and bandwidth) to the highest-impact opportunities.

- If possible, make the process visual, objective, interactive, and fun. Some teams place actual bets in "opportunity jars," vote with ballots or dots, create Lincoln-Douglas debates, and even play "Shark Tank" to establish their priorities. This creates a discrete, clear process, gets everyone involved, and can be high-energy. Be creative.

- With disagreements or conflicts, focus on logic and assumptions. If two or more people or groups see certain opportunities as high-priority and others don't, work hard to illuminate their differences in assumptions. If possible, focus on *why* they prioritize differently. Perhaps they disagree on the inherent value of an initiative, but more often, one is making assumption that the other is not. By embracing the contrast, the entire group deepens their own understanding of the potential opportunities and has a chance to strengthen their conviction.

Broad alignment by the team and critical stakeholders to the vision, the goals, and the associated priorities is crucial for the team to successfully implement changes, be they system repairs or capability enhancements. Leaders who are willing to ask the tough questions about how their team should function, often in the context of an off-site, will be ahead of the game and on their way to achieving alignment.

Selecting and adjusting the aperture of the conversation is a best practice that pays high dividends in results.

The next task at hand is to create a detailed plan to implement the highest-priority changes. That is the subject of chapter 8.

Chapter 7 Complexity Conqueror's Tactics

- Form a vision, be as specific and inspiring as possible, and let a broad group contribute to it so they "own" it.

- Think through what kind of a team is needed to achieve the vision and the long-term goals. Base it on how you score points.

- Treat off-site retreats as accelerating events (waypoints), not end-points. Use these events to accomplish a few critical tasks, avoid the laundry list, and allow plenty of time for the team to think, align and jell.

- Evaluate and prioritize opportunities for improvement in terms of how they will satisfy the vision.

- All along the way, ensure you are building alignment and commitment from the team and critical stakeholders on the overall approach, the priorities, and how to get there.

CHAPTER 8

CREATE THE PLAN

3-Stage Process, embedded risk mitigation, quick start, kickoff

When applying strategic change whilst fighting the Complexity Monster, it is critical to keep your options open and be nimble lest you over-commit to one approach and find yourself exposed, fighting on unenviable terrain.

Sun Tzu, in the 4th-Century B.C.E. work *The Art of War*, describes this important trait prior to entering battle. "There is no way for specific circumstances to be foretold. The intelligent general carefully examines his own methods prior to attacking a warlord. He is able to see the advantages of his immediate plans and the inherent dangers as well. By manipulating the conditions of his plan, he can overcome obstacles that he discovers when initiating the primary attack. By doing those things the fates will smile upon him."[13]

Armed with priorities, and an aligned team, it's time to create the

---

[13] Kaufman, Stephen F., and Tzu Sun. *The Art of War: The Definitive Interpretation of Sun Tzu's Classic Book of Strategy for the Martial Artist*. North Clarendon, VT: C.E. Tuttle, 2001, p. 69.

plan. At the same time, that plan cannot rely on only one method or approach. Indeed, multiple tactics are needed, and must also be ready to change as circumstances arise.

Brenda Facing Difficult Circumstances

Brenda is a feisty, well-liked executive at a large manufacturing firm. When she was a new executive, her first task from the big boss was to lead a critical initiative for the entire company. With more than $1 billion in new business on the line, she was under intense pressure to deliver, and the company was facing a set of volatile market dynamics they'd never experienced before.

To be successful, Brenda would need to elicit the cooperation of nearly every function across the 5,000-person company, and it was a mystery to her how she was going to accomplish it. When she asked for help, it was quickly apparent that this initiative would require every trick in the book. After working through the steps outlined in this chapter, Brenda navigated a difficult situation with high confidence.

After the planning and kickoff stage, she quickly gained traction. Avoiding crucial risk in advance, the team built major influence throughout the organization, ultimately finding success. In the end, she said, "It's incredible how much easier and more fun this initiative is since we planned it right, kicked it off well, and got the entire organization involved."

Planning for Priority Initiatives

In previous chapters, bets have been placed: bets on the future; bets (in the form of strategic change initiatives) that give the organization the highest possible chance to move toward its goals. But now, the rubber meets the road—*getting results.* For this, a killer plan is in order. For without a killer plan, the risk increases for each change project falling into the proverbial trash heap. But where to begin?

A good place to begin is to look at what factors typically keep most plans from ever gaining traction. These factors are, in no particular order:

- A lack of a clear value proposition: "What, in fact, is the benefit of this change, once successful?"

- A lack of rigorous thought about the actual approach to making the change

- A lack of appreciation and management of risk, regardless of approach

- An over-complicated or unfocused plan that is scattered and burdensome to manage

- A lack of clear measures (metrics) on the thing that is changing

- A lack of rigor in planning the logistical details such that the implementation team struggles to get started

- A perfect plan with imperfect resources and lackluster commitment by management to ensure success

There are other factors as well, but these are the ones seen most often.

Project Planning in Three Stages

To overcome these issues, experience suggests that asking the right questions in a strategic off-site or an in-house strategy session yields some of the best project plans. Break up the questions into three stages, while ensuring the questions from each stage are addressed satisfactorily before proceeding to the subsequent stage. Appendix B contains the complete set of questions for each of the three stages and is provided for reference.

▶ Stage 1 Questions

WHAT IS THE VALUE PROPOSITION OF THIS PROJECT?

"Value proposition" describes the benefit (or benefits) that accrue to the organization if the project were to be 100 percent successful. For example, if a manufacturer chooses to consolidate part types over a range of products in its catalog, it might realize benefits such as higher quality designs, leading to less rework in manufacturing, and larger volumes of fewer parts in the supply chain. This could lead to better inventory management, increase buying power, and provide room to lower prices so that it can trade margin or market share or both. If the team doesn't define the value proposition, then it runs the risk of leaving everyone

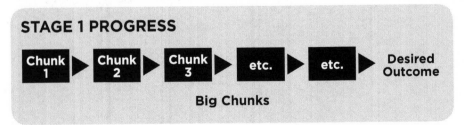

Stage 1 is about identifying major project elements to achieve the goal.

unfocused and fragmented, resulting in a lack of commitment in the heat of battle.

WHAT IS THE TEST FOR DONENESS?

This question allows the team to draw a finish line for the project. Just as a toothpick placed in a cake tests its doneness, it's critical to test for project doneness. The more specific, the better. As a rule, a good doneness test is a point at which the change initiative team can disband, the change will remain intact inside the organization, and the benefits will continue to accrue. For example, in an IT implementation, the doneness test might be: "The project is done when the software has been installed onto all user machines, all users have been trained, and have used the new system successfully for one month." That is clear.

Just as a toothpick placed in a cake tests its doneness, it's critical to test for project doneness.

WHAT ARE THE MAJOR CHUNKS OF THE PROJECT?

Instead of listing out all the detailed steps (that's coming), try instead to get a sense of the big-picture structure of the project. What are the major pieces? If a team is working with, yet struggling with, this concept, here's the simplest construct: assessment, synthesis, implementation. The key is to find up to five to seven major chunks. If there are more, the best advice is to combine chunks, or consider creating an additional project.

WHAT IS MY APPROACH?

This question is rarely asked because so many leaders have a mental default that there is only one way a change project should be run, and it's usually based on how they've done it in the past. However, experience, including that of Sun Tzu, suggests that successful teams consider multiple approaches at the outset. For example, to drive to the other side of a busy city, GPS navigation might give choices, such as "all freeways, all side streets, or all tolls." The actual choice might be based on traffic patterns in the area, the time of day, the day of the week, or even the weather. In Los Angeles, Thursdays tend to be the heaviest traffic day, while Fridays are often light. Thus, the routing choice made on Thursday might be different than on Friday. In a change project, choosing an approach such as "build it and they will come," "pilot, perfect, and scale," "big bang surprise," or the ever-popular "perfect it, build it, big bang surprise" (that one tends to go over well—*not*) is important. Smart teams evaluate the pros and cons to each approach before choosing a primary one.

Stage 1 Questions: Progress Check

Before moving to the next set of questions, look at the answers developed up to this point and ask a final question—is this project still worth doing? Can the team clearly see the benefits? Is the project structure clear? Is it clear when the project will end? Is there a defined approach being taken? If the answers are all *yes*, then move to the second stage of questions and enter a mode of more detailed planning. If not, keep working until all the answers are *yes*.

▶ Stage 2 Questions

This set of questions drives down into the details. Most teams start with this set, without doing the more fundamental work in the first set of questions. Many projects (read "bad bets") that shouldn't ever be started end up starting and unnecessarily taking up valuable time, money, and leadership bandwidth. Sound familiar? If the team hasn't asked the first questions, stop and go back to stage one.

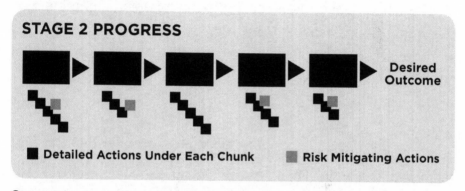

Stage 2 is about defining details and identifying risk.

WHAT ARE THE TOP THREE TO FIVE ACTIONS UNDER EACH CHUNK OF THIS PROJECT?

Remember the chunks? Those are the major sections of the project. Using whatever means the team prefers, write down the tasks that are the big hitters under each chunk. If one of the big chunks is "assessment," then the top actions could be to conduct focus groups, launch a survey, and analyze industry best practices. If another chunk is "pilot the solution," then the steps could be to identify the best spot for a pilot, draft the pilot plan, implement the pilot, then analyze the results. Repeat this approach for each chunk.

Once the team has listed three to five major steps under each chunk, it should have between fifteen and forty steps, depending on the level of detail. Avoid the temptation to identify more than sixty steps because that's the point where most projects begin to get too complicated. Someone will invariably want to place the steps into a whiz-bang software tool where it could (most often does) become lost forever.

WHAT ARE THE MAJOR RISKS?

A risk is the chance of something bad happening along the way that hasn't happened yet. Most often, typical risks include getting sidetracked to do other projects, a lack of reliable funding, a lack of buy-in from adjacent organizational stakeholders, a core solution that doesn't, in fact, work, etc. List as many risks as possible, and then prioritize them in terms of "likelihood of happening" and "severity if it happens."

Find the top few (yes, again, three to five).

WHAT STEPS CAN BE TAKEN TO PREVENT (OR MINIMIZE THE CHANCE OF) THESE RISKS OCCURRING?

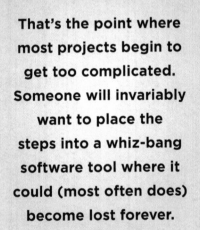

That's the point where most projects begin to get too complicated. Someone will invariably want to place the steps into a whiz-bang software tool where it could (most often does) become lost forever.

A simple example could be: Bob is walking in Seattle in the winter and there is risk that it will rain and he will get wet. Indeed, it is likely to rain there at that time of year, so perhaps Bob's mitigation step is to bring an umbrella. That makes the risk virtually go away, right? Another example is that a project team can have a lack of stakeholder buy-in and alignment. Lack of buy-in increases resistance to the change and makes the eventual outcome harder to achieve (and/or take longer). A mitigation step, discussed in chapter 7, could be to involve a stakeholder representative in the planning process up front, and focus on the value of the project that could accrue to her organization once the change is successful. Make a friend instead of creating an enemy. (By the way, this is one of the biggest risks encountered by change projects and one of the biggest mitigations that help.)

WHERE CAN PREVENTATIVE ACTIONS BE FOLDED BACK INTO THE PLAN?

For top risks, which mitigation steps can be placed back into the project plan? Under which chunk should the action occur? Once completed, the team ends up with a set of actions for the chunk, plus one or two or three risk-mitigation steps. Afterward, the severity and likelihood of occurrence of the major risks should be much lower.

WHO SHOULD LEAD THIS PROJECT?

Now is the time (if not sooner) to form an opinion about who the leader (or leaders) of this change should be. One guideline: the leader should be someone who has or who can marshal sufficient management bandwidth to focus his energy and the energy of the team on the project and its success. If not, then he should not be the leader. Perhaps sponsor, perhaps adviser, but not the leader. For major game-changing bets on the future, the leader needs to be in the game, on the field, but not in the bleachers.

Stage 2 Questions: Progress Check

At this point, you not only have a top-level concept for what you are trying to accomplish (stage one), but also up to sixty action steps that can be taken. Some of these include valuable preventative actions that reduce risk. Before moving to the final set of questions, look at the answers, and ask, "Is this project still worth doing? Do we see the path to the finish line? Is it realistic that with a committed, focused team, we can make this happen?" If the answers are all *yes*, then move to the third stage, and plan your logistics. If not, keep working until your answers are *yes* or you realize you need to abandon the project.

▶ Stage 3 Questions

This final set of questions is all about logistics and team operations. Answering these questions early prevents the team from stumbling out of the gate or never getting out of the gate in the first place. Here, the idea is to form initiative teams during the strategy session, have them sit together (with the leader having been chosen in the previous stage), and to write down answers to questions such as:

1. Where will we meet? How often?

2. Where will we store information?

3. Who else needs to be on the team?

Stage 3 answers critical questions so teams can start quickly.

4. What is our first expected quick win?

5. Who else needs to be on the team? (Again)

6. What's our standard agenda?

7. How many different types of meetings should we have?

8. Should we have a kickoff meeting to alert others of the project and elicit support?

9. Should we establish a standard dial-in number or virtual conferencing number?

10. Etc. (As previously noted, Appendix B contains an expanded list of questions for stages 1, 2, and 3)

As the group members complete the detailed questions, they make several decisions that will invariably begin to bring the plan into clear view. The team will gain confidence, and will want to start immediately.

But how to start? With small initiatives, a post-strategy session get-together to start is just fine. However, with larger initiatives involving several organizations or functions, a formal kickoff meeting is often the best solution.

PREPARING FOR A GOOD KICKOFF

A great game plan starts with a powerful kickoff. When the stakes are high and resistance possibly fierce, the right initiative done the right way can produce huge results. Implement the five approaches outlined here so that the team will be playing full out from the first to the last whistle.

WHAT DOES A SUCCESSFUL KICKOFF LOOK LIKE?

Every initiative starts off with a sketch of a vision that's been developed to implement and make work. There are a lot of details still missing, and those are critical to get clear before and during the kickoff.

START TO ADD COLOR TO THE SKETCH BEFORE THE KICKOFF ITSELF

Doing this informal work up-front can engage the team and motivate people to get on board quickly. Begin with the team's own ideas about what success looks like and how they will know that the initiative is complete. In other words, know where the goal posts are—the doneness test. Then build on and further improve those ideas by including input from management, the boss, customers and other stakeholders. Ask them to describe in detail how they, their teams, and their organization's performance could benefit if the initiative were successful. Use what is uncovered to further develop the vision.

WHAT'S THE KICKOFF PLAN?

The kickoff meeting (whether virtual, face-to-face, or a combination) is essentially a high-level planning session. Not surprisingly, an effective planning session requires a solid plan. First, consider what kind of conversational approach to use with the team. Sometimes a kickoff requires a narrow command-and-control aperture; other times, leaders want to open the conversational aperture to allow for a wider range of input and ideas.

CONSIDER WHO SHOULD BE ON THE TEAM

Make sure those important perspectives inside and outside the organization are represented. Upon deciding whom to include, develop tools and content to help guide and lead the session. An agenda (of course) is step one, and the leader may also want to create a visual presentation to focus the session and perhaps record the meeting. This content can serve to engage important participants.

HOW TO ELICIT THE BEST IDEAS

Not only does the kickoff set the tone for the entire initiative; it is also the time when ideas are the freshest and most unbounded. Don't miss this opportunity. During the kickoff, pay special attention to documenting, clarifying, and digging into the relevant issues and experiences of the team. Understand the stories each tells—their lessons, scars, and wisdom. Find ways to build their ideas into the implementation plan. Better yet, use those experts to help build that plan. When you open the aperture at this early stage, teams will emerge with better ideas, more seasoned approaches, and more involvement. Some of their stories might be excellent to inspire and mobilize the broader team down the road.

HOW TO BUILD IN RISK MITIGATION

There are several risks inherent in any initiative. The kickoff meeting is the perfect place to assess these risks and develop mitigation plans. Make sure the team is working on the right thing, that it has a flexible process to develop the optimal approach, and has also secured sufficient and appropriate resources and stakeholder buy-in. Lastly, don't expect the initial plan to be perfect. Adjust based on what is learned in the kickoff to create a plan that will serve as the baseline. Consider inviting others on the team to help refine the vision. Work multiple possible solutions in parallel until the team is confident the plan is sound. This takes more time in the beginning, but will ultimately deliver better outcomes.

HOW TO CREATE MOMENTUM

Success is determined at the kickoff and in the days, not weeks, following. Quickly move into execution mode immediately following the kickoff. Document action items, update the presentation, and share the plan and status with everyone, including the team and all stakeholders. Continue to communicate regularly, especially as progress is made, even if things get stalled. With a strong kickoff, the team is positioned to make significant, timely progress.

For initiatives, even complex ones, creating the plan does not need to be difficult. Indeed, often the clearest and most simple approaches win in the end. Taking the highest-priority initiatives through the Three-Stage Planning process, and adding a formal kickoff if needed, will avoid many of the typical failure modes experienced by leaders everywhere.

Chapter 8 Complexity Conqueror's Tactics

- Take the time to plan the highest-priority initiatives. Do it right.

- Avoid the temptation to go into too much detail too quickly. Use a three-staged approach to ensure the foundation is sound before framing the walls and hanging drywall.

- Keep the planning visible and flexible early on. Many great plans are lost forever in project management planning tools. Think in terms of five to seven major steps and twenty to thirty detailed steps (sixty max).

- Select the right leader and the right team to advise and support the initiative.

- Identify project risks and fold mitigation steps back into the plan.

- If a kickoff is required, use it to align the broader stakeholder group. Seek their ideas and get them on your side so they can help knock down inevitable barriers and cheer you on.

FOCUS EXECUTION
Prioritized implementation - Now, Next, Monitor

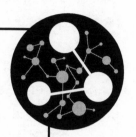

The Complexity Monster can sometimes manifest as *The Blob*, a classic creature from a 1958 Sci Fi thriller (remade in 1988). In the film, a meteor crashes to earth and starts off a chain of events that lead to a lifelike molten mass (the titular Blob) wreaking havoc on everything in its path. Feeding on everything it encounters, the Blob grows larger and hungrier until panic sets in. In time, the story's heroes discover that the Blob is vulnerable to cold temperatures. The townspeople eventually gather all the fire extinguishers in the town to blast cold at the monster, enough to pause it temporarily and transport it to the Arctic, where it allegedly remains dormant . . . but still alive today.

Organizations that launch too many initiatives at once often find they, as a mass, begin to take on a life of their own. They suck up all the management bandwidth, and, like the Blob, cause the destruction of everything in their path. In those situations, the complexity conqueror would do well to focus execution by placing less critical projects on ice to free up valuable space for the highest impact actions to progress quickly and finish. This then frees up the next set of projects to unfreeze and thrive.

Sam's Quest for Focus

Years ago, we had a client named Sam. Sam was an Ivy-league-educated PhD engineer who was articulate, sincere, and an up-and-comer within his corporation. At the same time, he'd been given leadership responsibility for a highly technical and much-maligned group that designed and procured critical technologies for spacecraft.

There were so many problems requiring so many changes he felt overwhelmed by the weight of it all. When he asked for help to figure out a plan and lead his leadership retreats, it was revealed that his group hadn't made much progress on the previous year's commitments. Knowing he needed to make some serious progress, we introduced a new concept to help.

For Sam and his team, it was a simple tool that helps to visually prioritize and authorize major organizational initiatives so they could focus on what was important and allocate their precious leadership bandwidth. After the first year of major progress, a much fleeter-footed Sam admitted, "This is so alarmingly simple. Isn't this how things should always be done?"

After several improvements and more than a decade later, this tool, dubbed *Now, Next, Monitor*, is used by the vast majority of our clients as a way to focus the execution of their strategic change efforts.

The Problem of Changing Too Much at Once

One of the biggest issues repeated time and time again is a well-meaning executive team with a basket of important change initiatives that, together or each on their own, either fix a systems issue or develop a new capability. Everyone will be initially excited and pumped up, and then the inevitable happens and the pressure of urgent daily operations overcomes the momentum of the project. Thus, initiative schedules bloat, project leaders get overwhelmed, and the change stalls. Often, halfway through the year when the leaders get back together, they realize their plight and concede, "Well, why don't we just cut it down a bit and at least get a win in one or two areas before the holidays?" In any event, the plan becomes a small shadow of its former self. Everyone reading this book has been there many times.

The following year, everyone recommits to do better, but the disappointment repeats. Ultimately, the inevitable question is, "Why can't we get more done?"

Why does this happen? There are at least three major causes of this phenomenon.

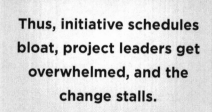

Thus, initiative schedules bloat, project leaders get overwhelmed, and the change stalls.

- **Limited Capacity:** An organization has only so much capacity (time, dollars, labor, leadership bandwidth, efficiency, etc.) to design, implement, and absorb change at once. And although this can often be increased, at any given moment in time, the plate is only so large.

- **Optimistic Estimates:** The capacity that an organization truly has is almost always overestimated. One reason for this is most leaders tend to be optimistic, which is a great and often crucial quality in a leader. However, in strategic change, it's often far overestimated. How often do you hear, "Gee Bob, we thought we could only get twelve initiatives done this year, but we did twenty instead"? How about never?

- **Thin Spreading of Bandwidth**: Of the capacity that truly exists, it is often spread out over many important simultaneous initiatives as opposed to deployed in a targeted and focused manner.

As a result, most initiatives either fade over the first several weeks, or the results they were supposed to achieve come later and are much weaker than hoped.

What is leadership to do? Admit the problem is impossible to solve? Seek a higher power? Phone a friend?

Experience suggests that at least part of the answer is found by studying previous productivity successes.

Applying Lean Principles to Managing Change

Over the past several decades, great strides have been made in manufacturing and service productivity in the United States and worldwide. By applying tools from W. Edwards Deming, Six Sigma, Lean, Dr. Eliyahu M. Goldratt's Theory of Constraints (TOC), and others, organizations have seen major strides in quality and productivity. In nearly all cases, there is one operation, be it a process or a machine, that governs the capacity of the entire system. As a simple example, in a bakery, the oven(s) are often the constraint. This means that the capacity of the oven determines the capacity of the entire bakery. So, in order to increase the bakery capacity, you don't need to make more dough or hire more people; you simply need to obtain more ovens or create recipes requiring less cooking time.

Throughout the past decade, we've witnessed some of our clients extending these concepts to the less rote, more artistic worlds of engineering design and testing and applying manufacturing philosophies to paper and CAD screens in order to improve quality and productivity and avoid costly mistakes and rework. Along the way, they have asked and answered the question, "What is the capacity of the engineer and the engineering team?"

Some successes have been remarkable, including multiple instances in which teams were consistently able to perform at a level of productivity between 30 and 50 percent higher than normal. In other cases, clients found that specific people with specific expertise (e.g., Stan, the only expert on technology X) are actually the constraint, and Stan's time needs to be seen as valuable currency.

Yet when it comes to managing strategic change, it's logical to extend the concepts of capacity and constraints even further. But in this case, instead of the machine or the expert engineer governing the capacity, ask, "What is the capacity of the leaders in the organization for change?" Essentially, this question is defining the "machine capacity" as the available leadership bandwidth for change.

Improving the Productivity of Strategic Change

In practical terms, five principled actions are necessary:

- **Principle 1—Manage Bandwidth:** Start by assuming that the chief constraint to initiative results is the bandwidth of leadership. The leader and the team are the constraint. Why? Because change initiatives have many moving parts, require a high degree of iteration, a high degree of "figure-it-out-ness," and plenty of check-ins with the chain of command and stakeholders across (or even outside) the organization. Change is a front-burner activity.

- **Principle 2—Start Small:** Because of Principle 1, start with a small number of projects, or even just one. Only when all the projects are making too much progress and everyone is leaving the office early out of sheer boredom is it permissible to add more, but not until then.

- **Principle 3—Win One in a Row:** Focus on the highest-impact project with the highest chance of success. Why? Most organizations have experienced the Flavor of the Day/Month/Year syndrome, in which a new, exciting initiative is proposed as "the thing that we are *really* going to do this time." Employees become increasingly weary and skeptical. They roll their eyes, are slow to get fired up, and conspire to wait it out until the fad fades or the boss leaves. But if leaders truly focus on one initiative, commit to it, and get a result,

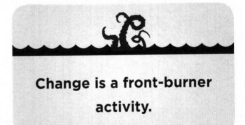

Change is a front-burner activity.

they can begin to build the confidence of the workforce and change this attitude.

- **Principle 4—Prepare.** Prepare the next initiative in advance of starting it. Think in terms of a cooking show, where all the ingredients are premeasured, the oven is turned on, and the previous dish is being enjoyed. Then, the cook/host simply turns to the camera and says, "Now we are going to make the main dish" and—voilà!—here are the ingredients and the hot pan, let's start. By doing it this way, preparing to start (some practitioners call this "full-kitting"), the chef is preparing to finish before she starts. Doing this enables the chef (or the team in this case) to go faster, with more focus because they aren't going to the store, or (like this author) searching endless cupboards for ingredients.

- **Principle 5—Maintain Visible Priorities.** Keep all the potential initiatives in full view and make priorities clear. For those important items that are not yet priorities, keep them on ice and authorize them only when you are confident the team has enough bandwidth to work the project and not before.

Using a Three-Bucket Tool Such as *Now, Next, Monitor*

At the beginning of this chapter, it was explained that, built from necessity in Sam's organization, the *Now, Next, Monitor* tool, or similar, implements the principles above and is specially tuned for teams that need to collectively prioritize and manage their strategic change initiatives. Dozens of organizations and their leadership teams have become insanely more productive using this simple tool.

The *Now, Next, Monitor* tool has three sections. Can you guess the three sections? Sure you can.

The *Now* section contains those few high-priority projects the team is working on now. The total demand of these tasks should equal or be less than the available management bandwidth in the organization for change. The leader knows the team has exceeded the available bandwidth if things slow down. If that happens, stop one initiative and place it into *Next*.

The *Next* section contains those initiatives that the team believes are valuable, but for which there is either not enough bandwidth to pursue immediately, or which logically require that another initiative be initiated first for it to be beneficial (e.g., the initiative to raise funds for the new building should come before the initiative to break ground on the new building, even if both are important). Items in the *Next* list are typically not planned in detail, but are scoped in terms of value, likely duration, overall approach, investment and other Stage 1 questions from chapter 8.

The *Monitor* section contains initiative candidates and ideas, and other forms of improvement. Over time, these items either make it to the *Next* or even *Now* list, or become extinct as "sounded like a good idea at the time." The main reason for the *Monitor* section is to ensure that all ideas can be heard and honored in a brainstorming session, while also keeping them visible and letting each reveal its inherent wisdom over time. This allows the organization to cultivate great ideas that were not observably great at the time they first arose (many great ideas are like that).

Implementation

The typical process of implementing *Now, Next, Monitor* is as follows. During an off-site or strategy session, there may be a dozen ideas about which the team wants to place their bets for the future. List these in the *Next* section. Then, in a structured conversation, allow the team to nominate specific initiatives for either the *Now* or the *Monitor* list. The first few are typically obvious. The biggest hitters will go to the *Now*, while the murky ideas with less potential for impact may go to *Monitor*. The rest stay in *Next*.

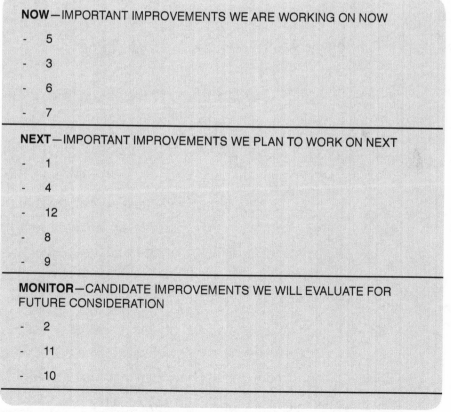

NOW—IMPORTANT IMPROVEMENTS WE ARE WORKING ON NOW

- 5
- 3
- 6
- 7

NEXT—IMPORTANT IMPROVEMENTS WE PLAN TO WORK ON NEXT

- 1
- 4
- 12
- 8
- 9

MONITOR—CANDIDATE IMPROVEMENTS WE WILL EVALUATE FOR FUTURE CONSIDERATION

- 2
- 11
- 10

How a typical set of 12 initiatives might fare after team discussions.

Often an idea or two might be combined and rescoped to better accommodate how the group forms its mental picture of the initiative. For example, two initiatives, one called "skill building" and one called "training," could be consolidated into a single initiative called "people development." This process continues until the group believes the list is stable and looks great. Here's a typical example of how an original list of twelve initiatives might fare.

Benefits of this Approach

Because it applies the principles mentioned earlier in this chapter, once the *Now, Next, Monitor* system is in place, the organization should expect to see the following benefits:

- The team is focused on only a few major, important initiatives.

- The organization doesn't take on too much and over-commit labor, time, or dollars.

- The teams have created a logical sequence or firing order between specific initiatives.

- Ideas not immediately embraced remain visible so that they can percolate; this also nurtures an environment in which people are more likely to bring up future ideas. This is a good thing, particularly in more complex organizations where multiple vantage points are crucial.

- The organization has a common language and lexicon (this is key) with which to discuss progress and adjust. For example, "Should we put this new idea in *Monitor* or *Next*?"

- High-priority initiatives get done faster and the organization improves faster.

- People feel more confident that the organization is making tangible progress and are more likely to embrace future changes.

Maintenance of the Tool

From vehicles to relationships, nearly everything valuable in life must be maintained. This process is no different. The following are critical aspects of *Now, Next, Monitor* maintenance.

First, assign someone to maintain the project list and keep it up to date. Some call it a Baseline or Current list, from which the group can make changes formally or informally.

Second, decide the criteria from which to make changes. We suggest using at least two types of changes: Major (type I), and Minor (type II):

- **Major (type I):** These are changes to the objective, scope, approach, duration, budget, or leader of a project. This type also applies when a project is determined to be complete or for some reason is out-prioritized and moved back to *Next* or even *Monitor.* Type I changes should be decided by a governance committee (see chapter 11 on governance).

- **Minor (type II):** These are changes to the title, team members, detailed plan, and other administrative items. Type II changes can be often administered less formally by the person maintaining the *Now, Next, Monitor* process.

Third, create a forum or meeting, at least monthly, to review progress of the initiative projects. Carefully consider the progress the projects are making in terms of the plan created in the previous chapter. It is important to keep track of the type I items on each initiative to avoid inevitable drift. By requiring type I changes to be approved by the governance committee, leaders are essentially tying mooring lines to the projects, allowing them room to move with the current and tides, but keeping them secure—not too loose and not too tight. Without the mooring lines, the project can easily drift out to sea or onto jagged rocks. A best practice is to have a monthly "light" (less comprehensive) review and a quarterly "heavy" (more comprehensive) review. But each project is different in terms of its maturity and intensity; thus, the leader needs to use judgment, and real progress trends to decide the frequency of review.

Fourth, in a regular forum, in addition to evaluating each individual initiative, also look at the collective set. Are the initiatives progressing? Are there a lot of type I changes? Is the quantity of projects in the *Now* too large (meaning the management bandwidth capacity has been exceeded by the set of projects)? If regular progress is being made on the entire set, great. Continue. If not, consider freezing a project (or a portion of a project) and moving it to the *Next* until another project in the *Now* completes, thus freeing up valuable bandwidth and resources.

Declaring Victory on an Initiative

Hopefully, if the initiative has been done right, the team will have focused and finished a project, achieved its doneness test, and will be enjoying the value proposition benefits. Remember the IT example? At this point the organization now has a shiny new IT system in place and everyone is trained and using the system productively. This is the time to declare victory! After a project is completed, teams will typically remove it from the *Now* list (it's done), and either continue with the remaining projects in the *Now* or consider whether an additional project can be moved up from *Next* to *Now*. The team governance process should help determine the right answer here.

Management bandwidth is difficult to measure. To determine how much one has, it's best to assume one has very little. Then, over time, continue to add load until things begin to slow. Like in weight training, best to start with lighter weight than start too heavy and risk a muscle tear. Build upon success.

Management bandwidth is difficult to measure. To determine how much one has, it's best to assume one has very little. Then, over time, continue to add load until things begin to slow. Like in weight training, best to start with lighter weight than start too heavy and risk a muscle tear. Build upon success.

Now that great project plans are in place, and the *Now, Next, Monitor* system is up and running and focusing execution, it's time to build a roadmap and see how all the changes fit together to support the vision and long-term goals.

Chapter 9 Complexity Conqueror's Tactics

- Study the concept of management bandwidth as a constraint.

- Make a commitment to take on only the small set of changes that can be done successfully, and delay other initiatives that can or should start later.

- Adopt a three-bucket visible prioritization tool like *Now, Next, Monitor* and use it to manage the focus of the organization on priority system fixes and capability improvements.

- Facilitate a discussion with the leadership team on what items should be done *Now, Next,* or be put into *Monitor.*

- Assign someone with the responsibility to keep the *Now, Next,* and *Monitor* list fresh and accurate.

- Create a forum that meets regularly where changes to the baseline can be discussed and incorporated into the *Now, Next, Monitor* lists.

- Declare victory when an initiative is complete. Bask in the spoils and move up another item onto the *Now* list if capacity exists. Stick with it, and it will soon become a routine part of your rhythm (weekly, monthly, and quarterly).

CONSTRUCT THE ROADMAP

Strategic Improvement Roadmap, built right-to-left

Roadmaps can be immensely valuable, especially when they come in the form of a treasure map.

In his 1883 novel, *Treasure Island*, Robert Louis Stevenson weaves an adventure tale of swashbuckling pirates in search of hidden treasure that details the bloody mutiny (yes, another mutiny) on the ship *Hispaniola*. In the story, Captain Smollett is in sole possession of the map to a hidden treasure on a distant island. This fact lures the crew, led by one-legged cook Long John Silver, into a bloody rebellion. They take the map and keep the treasure for Cook's mutineers and himself.

As in all quest stories, the treasure map lit the path to the treasure. But what if they didn't have a map? Would they have even begun the journey? How much more in the dark would the voyage have been without it? The map was the key.

As with a fictional treasure map, a well-designed strategic roadmap sheds light onto the transformation path, and clarifies the journey that leads to the treasure of ROI. And although one hopes no one will "kill" for access to your map, it's likely that as you construct the roadmap, you will attract many interested parties clamoring to be a part of your expedition, relieved at the clarity it provides.

Returning to Anthony's Roadmap

At the start of the book, Anthony's SOS moment came when he was lambasted by the military brass and told that he and his team needed to ensure the government's "mission coursed through every vein in their body" or he couldn't be trusted. Anthony ultimately created a real ROI situation and turned his program profits from zero percent to near 100 percent in just a few quarters.

And although Anthony's team used many of the techniques in this book, they also gained huge leverage through using a strategic improvement roadmap they dubbed the "Program Path to Excellence." This roadmap served as a guidepost for his diverse set of supplier and customer stakeholders and galvanized every organization around supporting Anthony's plan. Using the roadmap, Anthony and his leaders could demonstrate leadership, provide vision, and inspire an extremely complex program team toward huge success.

At this point, you have a set (typically eight to twelve) of improvement initiatives that have been scoped, prioritized, and placed into a three-bucket tool like *Now, Next, Monitor.* If you have gotten this far, congratulations. At this point, a second tool that extends from the previous one can take improvement efforts to the next level. This tool is called a *Strategic Improvement Roadmap,* or SIR.

What Is a Strategic Improvement Roadmap (SIR)?

A SIR is a time-phased, logic-based, simple, visual depiction of the major improvement efforts, how they relate to one another, and how they individually and collectively support the vision and long-term goals.

This roadmap served as a guidepost for his diverse set of supplier and customer stakeholders and galvanized every organization around supporting Anthony's plan.

WHAT PROBLEM DOES IT SOLVE?

- Creating it forces the team to make a lot of decisions about how the improvement will be conducted, because the interrelationships need to be sorted out.

- It is a powerful communication tool for all stakeholders, including employees, customers, suppliers, management, and investors.

- It can serve as a strong baseline from which to evaluate changes and new ideas. Each one needs to earn its way onto the roadmap.

- It becomes a powerful and meaningful way to elicit perspective and feedback from the set of diverse participants with diverse vantage points, which are critical in a complex organization.

Key Elements of a Strategic Improvement Roadmap

A good roadmap has the following major features:

- An inspiring title that means something to the stakeholder audience

- Summary of the vision and major long-term goals of the organization

- All the major change initiatives critical to achieving the goals (think *Now* and *Next* initiatives), each having a start, duration, completion and major project milestones

- A time horizon of twelve to sixty months (more typically eighteen to thirty-six months) so multiple years of planning can be considered at once

- An accountable name associated with each initiative; typically, the initiative leader or her boss who is ultimately accountable for its successful completion (better to have a specific person versus an organization or function; both are OK)

- Essential relationships between the initiatives; this is often a dependency that one cannot start before the previous one is completed (e.g., paint only after you prime and let dry).

- Simplicity; although the roadmap contains a lot of information, once that information coalesces, it can be shown in a simple form that is visually appealing (If it requires a PhD and hours to study and understand it, then it's too complicated.)

A basic example of a roadmap is below.

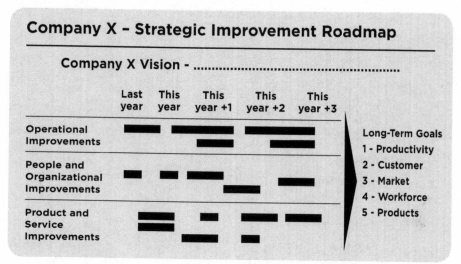

A popular example of a strategic improvement roadmap.

Roadmaps can come in many shapes and formats and styles. Good ones, however, include most of the characteristics above. Leaders should play around with different formats and styles to find something that works and can be maintained. The best roadmaps, regardless of form, keep the depiction simple and digestible for a broad audience.

Using a Roadmap

Just as one can't drive cross-country in one moment, an organization can't implement their entire roadmap all at the same time. There is a sequence, a journey, a method to the madness.

Roberta, a detail-oriented, driven leader, led a testing organization that was always in the spotlight. In her operation, a single wasted day could cost millions of dollars in profit to her parent company. Smart, she realized she needed to ensure that everyone in her global organization knew the plan for improvement. When she built her Strategic Improvement Roadmap, she included major sections such as People, Processes, Tools, and Infrastructure to ensure that each of her two-dozen facilities played from the same sheet of music. Each month, she held a leadership strategy meeting, reviewed the status of each initiative and updated her *Now, Next, Monitor* list with discipline and precision. Roberta was a pace-setter for her industry peers and when asked if the roadmap was instrumental to her success, she quipped, "I don't know how we ever lived without it."

Common Practical Uses

Once the roadmap is in place, it can be used to gain further alignment and clarity both inside and outside the organization. It can also provide a context from which to evaluate changes. Additional ways to use a roadmap include:

- Make it visible. Post it in common areas, on internal (or external if appropriate) websites.

- Explain it often, and teach the entire organization to study it and suggest ways of making it better and clearer.

- Have the executive team practice explaining the roadmap to each other from their own vantage point; this helps bring it to life and can be extremely powerful.

- Use it in all presentations to set the context. For example, "Given where we are going overall, here's what I want to discuss today and how the topic fits in."

- Use it to evaluate changes to the plan. If you see a change in context of the bigger picture, you are less likely to make a suboptimal decision.

- Connect it to your *Now, Next* list. Some groups consider projects in the current and following quarter as *Now*, and anything beyond that as *Next*.

- Use it to tell a story of past, present, and future, with rationale for choices.

- Build a communications package or presentation with the roadmap and each of the major initiatives on subsequent pages. Put this content on a website.

Leaders who take their most critical strategic initiatives and build a roadmap that depicts each change in a sequential, connected, and logical manner are ahead of the game in terms of their ability to powerfully communicate their vision, strategy, and means to get there. That allows them leverage in influencing employees and stakeholders to support the plan and is the first line of defense against inevitable corporate antibodies that seek its destruction.

Chapter 10 Complexity Conqueror's Tactics:

- Assign a small team to spend the time required to build the roadmap, including the incorporation of feedback from the broader team, stakeholders, etc.

- Keep the roadmap at a high level, showing the small set of change initiatives with title, duration, accountable leader, and start-stop expectations. Avoid the temptation to fill in too much detail, making it too complicated.

- Make the long-term objectives visible so that it is clear how the change initiatives support those objectives.

- Avoid the temptation to make your roadmap into a detailed spreadsheet. The top-level thematic view provides the sweet spot of situational thinking without getting bogged down in mechanics. It's part art and part science. Embrace the tension.

- Plan to reference the roadmap often as a backdrop for context every time you or your team communicates to stakeholders.

- Keep the roadmap visible, allowing everyone easy access to the latest version. Make it available as an online reference, place it in standard presentations, etc.

SECTION

3

Managing the SOS2ROI Portfolio

Introduction to Section III

While the previous section dealt with the seven fundamental steps and techniques in the SOS2ROI approach (the car), this section addresses how to develop an environment and culture in which SOS2ROI techniques can thrive when multiple initiatives (a portfolio) are involved. Not just once, but year after year. Like any smooth track, these elements can help you minimize complexity and friction and get results faster. In discussing the final step, *Manage the Portfolio* (step 8), two critical elements are considered:

- **Chapter 11: Architecting the Management System**— these are the structures and processes the organization must have in place to build, sustain, and improve its change portfolio year after year.

- **Chapter 12: Maintaining Speed**—these are the skills you need to master in order to shield and counter the inevitable corporate antibodies that will conspire to derail you and your team from charting your best course and sticking with your plan. Consider this the advanced guide.

CHAPTER 11

Architecting the Management System

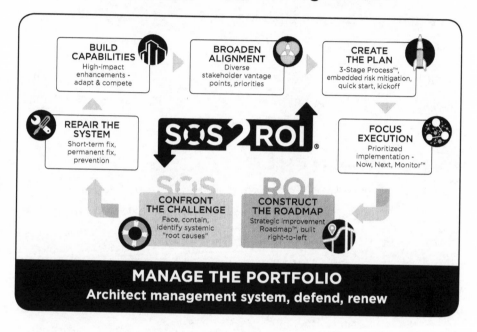

As previously discussed, doing battle with a monster that has one head is difficult enough. But, how should the conqueror proceed if the monster is multiheaded?

According to Greek mythology, Hercules had to confront this challenge by defeating the Hydra, a gigantic water-snake monster with nine heads, one of which was immortal. Anyone who attempted to behead the Hydra found that as soon as one head was cut off, two more heads would arise directly from the fresh wound.

To succeed in conquering this multiheaded monster, Hercules enlisted the aid of his nephew, Iolaus. The two of them developed a system. As Hercules severed each of the Hydra's mortal heads, Iolaus's job was to the cauterize each fresh wound with fire so that no new heads would emerge. When only the immortal head remained, Hercules cut it off, too, and buried it securely under a heavy rock.

Having mastered the SOS2ROI process for a single change, the next step—managing multiple changes—requires an advanced set of tactics. It requires architecting the management system.

Terry's Nine-Headed Monster

As a newly promoted VP at a multinational aerospace firm, Terry, a sincere, hardworking, honest son of a Midwestern farmer, began what he knew was to be an intense journey. His bosses had charged him with integrating nine distinct operational entities under a newly created product testing group, for which he would be accountable. Like buying and combining nine companies at once, Terry was confronted daily with organizational complexity, diverse and oft-conflicting cultural forces, and danger lurking around every turn.

Terry's challenge was threefold. First, he needed to realize a corporate mandate to save money from the combined organization: a number so large it had many zeros and more than two commas. Second, he had to bring together the groups in such a way that they could function more efficiently so that the value of the services increased. And third, like overhauling the engine while speeding down the freeway, he needed to do both while also running these nine business groups without a hitch, handling daily execution and keeping his customers happy.

Determined, Terry asked us to lend a hand to help conquer the complexity and facilitate the transition. During the next several quarters, Terry and his team used their diversity as a strength and leveraged the vantage points of each of the members to align around a small set of objectives, along with a roadmap they could all commit to. Along the way, we architected a management system that allowed them to routinely sense and adapt to new insights and changes in their business and environment to keep on track.

Ultimately, the organization embraced nearly every aspect of SOS2ROI and has learned to perform well as a matter of habit. Terry's insight? By creating a management system, we slashed through the thickets and emerged on the other side stronger and wiser.

Establishing a Management System

After covering the essential (at times iterative) steps for creating a strategic initiative to either repair a system issue or create a new capability, it's time to explore a management system for change. With a management system, the leader effectively creates an enabler for multiple initiatives (typically those in *Now,* and *Next*) to thrive. This is called "Managing the Portfolio."

The Importance of Governance

Imagine air travel with no air or ground control. Each pilot could take off when he felt like it, fly at any elevation, take any route, decide how much fuel to carry, and land at whichever runway he chose. Mayhem would ensue. Heading home for the holidays?

You wouldn't be able to tell anyone exactly when you were leaving, when you'd land, or if you'd be alive when you got there. That's why there is an air traffic control system with a set of rules and procedures that coordinate and govern the safety, efficiency, and predictability of air and airport traffic.

Similarly, if the initiatives in your *Now* and *Next* list can fly off in any direction, then you are inviting trouble. Your projects will be inefficient, likely in conflict (if not colliding), and time, dollars, energy, and value will be wasted along the way.

Limited Governance Is OK

For each project, there is a portion that should be standardized and another portion that should be more customized. How much is under governance depends on various factors, including the maturity of the strategic management process, the culture of the organization, the strength and depth of the administrative support, and the personalities, preferences, and experience of the leaders. Thus, how much governance you apply is ultimately a judgment call. Too much governance and the initiative teams may feel stifled, may not innovate, or may not create to their potential. By contrast, too little governance and you have mutiny and chaos on your hands.

Too much governance and the initiative teams may feel stifled, may not innovate, or may not create to their potential. By contrast, too little governance and you have mutiny and chaos on your hands.

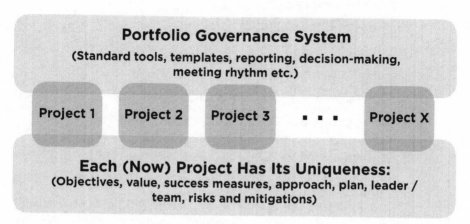

Leaders need to strike a balance between centralized insight and decentralized execution.

Components of a Management System

Although many options exist for what a management system could look like, the following are minimum components:

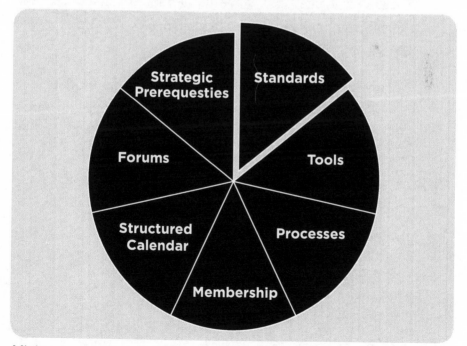

Minimum components of a good strategic management system.

- **Strategic Prerequisites**: These are items that every organization needs as a basis for improving performance. These include but are not limited to vision, mission (and/or purpose/identity) of the organization, long-term goals (three to five years), and shorter-term goals (one to two years).

- **Standards**: These might include planning methodologies (e.g., Three-Stage Planning process), methods and formats for reporting, common terminology, and a stable process for managing change.

- **Tools**: It is helpful if everyone is using the same tool set, which might include strategic analysis frameworks (such as SWOT, Porter's Five Forces), team and individual assessment instruments (such as Myers-Briggs, Birkman, DiSC), and strategic implementation tools such as the *Three-Stage Planning* process, *Now, Next, Monitor* and *Strategic Improvement Roadmap*.

- **Forums**: These are standing advisory and/or decision-making groups/committees that use the tools and apply the standards to advise the individual initiatives, make decisions on priorities, allocate resources (e.g., time, dollars, bandwidth) remove roadblocks, and fine-tune.

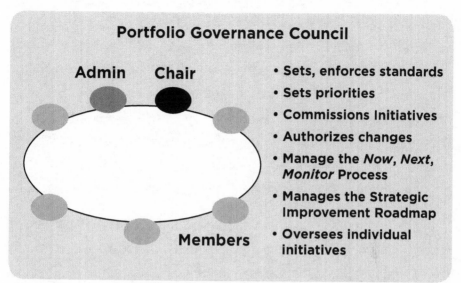

A Portfolio Governance Council is an example of a regular forum.

- **Structured Calendar**: This is a schedule of routine times during which the strategic groups conduct their activities. Typically, there is a weekly meeting to discuss changes and remove roadblocks, a monthly session, a quarterly session, and an annual session. Each of these is a chance to update the plan, reprioritize if needed, declare victory on successes, and commission new efforts.

With these components in place, the organization can begin to manage its strategic improvements as a process instead of the more typical five- or ten-year plan that collects dust on the shelf.

Habits of Successful Strategic Management Systems

Over time, as organizations implement a mature strategic management system, certain success habits form. At least three habits of successful strategic management systems are worth noting.

HABIT 1: *USE GATES TO INVEST SMARTLY*

Successful leaders think like an investor in their improvement projects and consider three sources of capital: people (bandwidth), time, and dollars. As with most investments, the goal is to minimize risk and management cost while maximizing returns (ROI). Unfortunately, too many leaders overinvest in a project before its true value can be assessed. Feeling pressure to get on with it, they go all-in and take on too much risk prematurely and unnecessarily.

Instead, set up your projects in stages, with gates between each stage. For example, stages might include: concept, assessment, synthesis, planning, experimentation, and execution. And in between each stage, there is a gate or check-in to ensure the previous stage is complete and the project is still relevant and ready to head to the next stage.

It's akin to renting a car. Before leaving the airport, there is a gate that is closed prior to you driving the car off the lot. The agent at the booth checks the contract and your driver's license, and if it all checks out, then and only then opens the gate to allow you to pass by. The same concept can apply to projects. Instead of releasing all funds, authorize courses of action incrementally using gates along the way that correspond to accomplishments. Often called milestones, these accomplishments trigger the opening of a previous constraint (or gate) that enables the project to move forward.

As an example, in the case of venture funding, once milestones are achieved in a business plan, additional funds are released to be applied to specific projects, enabling the next level of growth. For example, the investor may be happy to invest in a franchise idea, but may want to perfect the original prototype in a test market prior to approving multiunit expansion.

HABIT 2: *INSTALL RUMBLE STRIPS TO MANAGE DRIFT*

You've been there. It's late at night, you are driving down an endless stretch of highway, windows down, mega-cup of truck-stop coffee in your hand as you fight drowsiness. Then, suddenly, you are startled by a *"bump, bump, bump"* vibration and patter, alerting you that you have drifted to the edge of the lane. Adrenaline courses through your veins and you immediately awake and readjust— heart beating a thousand times a second.

Strategic projects can also drift. Often because they are over-whelmed by the urgency of daily operational responsibilities, project managers actively or passively learn how to "game" the system and allow certain project elements to "drift" away from their original intent. This phenomenon is often subtle and, therefore, difficult to detect. Examples are changes (usually reductions) in project scope, increasing timelines, reductions in the magnitude of expected results, and even changes to the approach. Is this done out of malice? No.

As an example, in the case of venture funding, once milestones are achieved in a business plan, additional funds are released to be applied to specific projects enabling the next level of growth.

It's often simply because the leader discovers she lacks the band-width to execute the original scope as designed. If discovered, it's typically later in the year and the boss says, scratching her head, "Did I approve that change?"

So, what's the big deal? Managers are busy, right? The big deal is that if this behavior pervades, then the organization can't determine how much available bandwidth capacity it truly has. And bandwidth, as discussed extensively in this book, is often the constraining factor to project success. A good understanding of bandwidth helps decision-making in terms of what items can be in the *Now* list. If projects unknowingly drift, then the organization could falsely believe it has enough bandwidth to add *more* projects. The reality, however, is that the projects on the current *Now* list have simply drifted away from their original scope and now *demand* less bandwidth.

To combat this, rumble strips need to be installed to trigger certain responses and ensure they are managed by the governance process. Typically, changes to budget or schedule (time) are managed, but it's also important to manage other items, such as project scope, project approach, and even the makeup of the project team. For example, if a project manager found that his team was working nights and weekends, instead of addressing it, she would change the duration of the project from six months to seven or eight months and communicate to management that everything is on track. If management had not set up a governance system, then this would go unnoticed, but the timing of the ultimate value creation could be severely delayed.

If this behavior pervades, then the organization can't determine how much available bandwidth capacity it truly has.

Rumble strips on more than just cost and schedule reveal bandwidth challenges and force discussion and decisions on how they should be addressed.

HABIT 3: *HANDLE CHANGES TO SAVE BANDWIDTH*

Early in this chapter, Terry embarked on a quest to integrate several organizations. Along this journey, he realized he had not only inherited nine different organizations, but also nine different ways of doing literally everything. And to top it off, each organizational leader was convinced his approach was the best and fervently resisted letting go. Like a nine-headed monster, this created an overwhelming sense of bureaucracy, confusion, and frustration for anyone trying to get anything done within the organization. Through our working together, Terry's leaders decided to confront the monster, removing complexity by creating an initiative to identify the best-of-breed processes in a way that each organization could participate in evaluating, selecting, and finally adopting the best version, to eliminate redundancy and simplify the workload.

The approach was to survey each organization's portfolio of processes for product testing and choose the process that would be the *gold standard* for all organizations to use. As the team was implementing this survey approach, it became apparent that each organization not only had different kinds of processes, but also a singularly distinct way of *organizing* its processes. When this was presented to the strategic forum, the team was directed to pause the survey effort and, instead, focus on building a common process architecture. Like a Dewey Decimal system for library classification, this architecture enabled each process to be evaluated in terms of how it fit within the standard list. This change to project approach was approved by the strategic council and implemented successfully.

Thus, the survey effort could accelerate, and the initiative team was ultimately able to remove more than half of the duplicative processes while significantly reducing bureaucracy and confusion (an example of conquering the Complexity Monster by simply removing non-value-added complexity). The lesson learned for Terry and his team was that often, changes to a project's approach, while disruptive, are necessary to achieve success. His governance system helped him to sense there was a problem, and to develop and implement a solution quickly to avoid wasteful dead-ends and keep the project on track.

To summarize, architecting a system to manage the change portfolio creates the space for issues to arise, priorities to be managed, and corrective action to be taken. The most effective systems can also cultivate a sense of cohesion within even the most diverse organizations, enabling them to use their differences as an advantage.

Chapter 11 Complexity Conqueror's Tactics:

- Set up a small team or individual to administer the SOS2ROI tools (e.g., *Now, Next, Monitor, Strategic Improvement Roadmap,* and project plans for each initiative).

- Form a strategic governance council that meets regularly to review the status of the initiatives in the *Now* list, handle potential major changes, help remove roadblocks, make decisions, and move items from *Next* to *Now* (or vice versa) when appropriate.

- Set up a strategic routine with a monthly, quarterly, semiannual, and annual cycle, so that you are running your strategic improvements as a process. Mix in virtual meetings with face-to-face meetings if the team is geographically distributed.

- Install rumble strips to ensure projects don't drift off their original intent without a discussion about how the change might impact the portfolio.

- Give your team permission to stop, regroup, and make a change to an initiative if the original plan is less than ideal.

CHAPTER 12

Maintaining Speed

In this book, an array of tools and techniques has been presented for managing strategic change while conquering the Complexity Monster. The previous chapter upped the game a bit by describing the kind of management system required to routinely handle multiple simultaneous changes.

Stepping back, it's wise to acknowledge that no one leader, no one complexity conqueror, will or should be able to implement all this advice at once. As an astute leader, you should select the tools and techniques that apply best to the situation at hand so that you can focus and get quick results without getting bogged down.

Of course, that is easier said than done. Consider some wisdom from philosopher Friedrich Nietzsche, who warned, "Whoever fights monsters should see to it that in the process he does not become a monster. And if you gaze long enough into an abyss, the abyss will gaze back into you."[14] Learn and practice a few tools of the complexity conqueror at a time. This will give you your best chance at accelerating results, and then maintaining speed.

Protecting What's Important

Just as a homeowner installs security systems and takes other precautions to protect his home from intruders, so too must the

---

[14] Nietzsche, Friedrich. *Beyond Good and Evil—Prelude to a Philosophy of the Future*. Aphorism 146.

strategic leader take precautions to protect those important plans and priorities that will bring success.

Managing "Incoming!"

In battle, when a mortar is headed your way, the appropriate response is to yell "incoming!"

One of the primary risks to a healthy strategic management system (where initiatives are planned, prioritized, and implemented to achieve strategic objectives to achieve high ROI) is pressure from multiple sources to do something different. This pressure can come in many forms.

- Pressure from bosses or customers to do something differently
- Pressure from external or even peer organizations who have their own agendas or opinions
- Pressure from pet projects that come from managers inside the leader's own organization
- Deprioritized activities that somehow remain active
- Completed initiatives that should be over, but somehow continue
- Overreacting to a new piece of singular data (such as a negative report)
- And more

The impact of these pressures, if acted upon, is that the improvement plan becomes degraded, priorities become opaque, complexity takes over, and the team loses confidence.

Transformation plans are vulnerable and must be protected.

PROTECTING PROJECT X

Richard, a go-getter with a charismatic personality, had just taken over a large central product engineering organization that was getting a bad rap and was in desperate need of a rebirth. Product designs were taking too long, problems in testing and in the field were causing expensive recalls, and most (if not all) of those problems could be traced back to risky and incomplete engineering designs.

Not only was the organization struggling, but repeated failed attempts to improve the situation had driven many of the product division leaders to write off and lose faith in the engineering teams who supported them, and build expensive rogue teams inside their business units.

Never one to back away from a challenge, Richard knew he had to do something significant, not only to fix the product problems, but also to restore confidence and credibility that the group could once again be trusted. To his credit, Richard was a leader who had built his success by surrounding himself with top-notch talent, whether inside or outside the organization.

He brought us in to work with his top leaders to devise and implement a strategy to break through the challenge and revitalize the organization.

Over a series of weeks, the group uncovered the root causes and built a solution dubbed Project X. Richard and his team were sure it would be a real winner with a serious chance of success. He chartered the idea, built the plan and team to flesh out the details, and began implementation.

Yet that's when the challenges *truly* started.

Since the engineering group had had many previous false starts at improvement, there was a degree of reluctance to take on the project fully, so some leaders within the organization advocated additional projects in addition to Project *X*. Also, several peer organizations, such as operations, quality, and finance—playing Monday-morning quarterback—had other ideas about how to "fix" engineering. Working with a team of his executives, we helped Richard implement several tactics designed to incubate the rebirthing organization and allow Project *X* to thrive.

The first tactic was to limit the "incoming" from the internal team by building a stop-and-freeze list. Instead of discontinuing all the noncritical projects, he worked with the organization to determine the right timing for each, putting them on pause or freeze in the interim to be reviewed at a future date. Others he stopped (deleted) altogether.

The second was to limit the "incoming" from external and peer organizations (such as operations, quality, and finance) that had opinions about what else engineering should be doing. Here, Richard assigned individual leaders to be the singular point of contact or liaison to those organizations. Like sentries, these liaisons provided early warning on incoming obligations of lower priority which could then be diverted away from the Project X team.

Third, Richard installed a team to manage all the additional incoming threats to Project X and allow it to thrive. Like a secret service for Project X, this team reviewed new requests for non-Project-X work on a weekly basis and polled all the leaders in the organizations on anything that could derail the focus on Project X.

Because of these tactics, Project X blossomed. In less than a year, not only had it achieved significant cost savings for the business units, but it was also endorsed by the CEO and implemented well beyond engineering. Throughout the experience, Richard and his team learned that to focus, sometimes you must actively combat those shiny things that might tempt you to *lose* focus, especially in the delicate stages of rebirth.

Learning How to *Stop* and *Freeze:* It's Not as Easy as You Think

In *Good to Great*, James C. Collins wrote:

> Good is the enemy of great. And that is one of the key reasons why we have so little that becomes great. We don't have great schools, principally because we have good schools. We don't have great government, principally because we have good government. Few people attain

great lives, in large part because it is just so easy to settle for a good life.[15]

In any SOS2ROI transformation, many good ideas can be generated, and that is a great aspect of the process. At the same time, not all of these ideas are worth focus, at least not at first. Yet somehow, once leaders get a project going, like a freight train, it can be difficult to stop. Experience dictates that to stop an initiative to make room for a better one, more than a memo or decree is required.

STOPPING AN INITIATIVE

Initiatives you want to stop behave almost like that villain our hero is attempting to defeat at the end of the thriller movie. Be it the shark in *Jaws*, the borderline fan in *Play Misty for Me*, or the T1000 liquidmetal killing machine in *Terminator 2*, a monster is notoriously difficult to kill. You think he's done for, and the hero lets his guard down and (always) turns his back on the villain who then (always) miraculously wakes up again and takes another run. The hero defeats the villain again, but did he really? When is the monster truly done for?

This is also true of strategic initiative projects. But why? This happens, in part, due to the following reasons:

- **Personal investment:** People are personally devoted, have put in a lot of time and energy and don't want to say goodbye.

- **Habits are hard to break:** The implementation team is in the habit of working together, showing up to the same conference room or daily phone call.

[15] Collins, James C. *Good to Great: Why Some Companies Make the Leap...and Others Don't.* New York, NY: Harper Business, 2001, p. 1.

- **Infrastructure momentum:** No one closes the charge account or changes the cipher lock on the conference room door.

- **Simple denial:** The team doesn't believe the initiative is stopped. "It's OK; I'm sure the boss will change her mind."

- **Fear of loss:** Team members may not know what their next assignment will be and, due to fear, continue working in hopes that the project will be revived.

- **Convenience of rebranding:** The team finds a way to associate the old stopped initiative with one that remains approved or on the *Now* list. If successful, they can resume right where they left off but under a new mantle.

You think he's done for, and the hero lets his guard down and (always) turns his back on the villain who then (always) miraculously wakes up again.

Like a good hero, the leader must not let his guard down, but instead keep at it to ensure that the villain is truly slain. Tactics that are best practices include:

- Visibly and clearly communicate the decision that the initiative is stopped. Put it in writing and place it on a stop list. Some clients have added *Stop* to *Now, Next, Monitor*, so that employees see visibly that the initiative is no longer active. If controversial, explain the rationale for the decision and formally thank the team for their efforts. If there are clear benefits that have been accrued, indicate those as well.

- Close charge lines and deny approval of expenses that are linked to the project after the date the project was stopped.

- Delete all meeting notices, including reports to the governance council, reporting status to bosses, and all project team meetings.

- Reassign personnel, hopefully to a higher-priority initiative so that their focus is on building something new, and not on perpetuating the stopped project.

- Restrict access to the project archives, either on a shared site or shared drive that the project team utilized for storing work product and managing the project.

- Create a small event to celebrate or reward the accomplishments of the team and thank them for their efforts. Explain the rationale behind stopping the project, and express how much their time, talent, and dedication is appreciated. This can serve to give the team a sense of closure and is another highly visible indication that it's time to move on.

FREEZING AN INITIATIVE

Like stopping, freezing (or pausing) an initiative puts it aside for a future date but, in the case of freezing, does not delete (dispose of) it. Although some of the same challenges exist in freezing and stopping, the focus on freezing is having a successful re-start once the initiative is thawed.

CHALLENGES IN RESTART

There are often challenges when restarting a frozen initiative.

- The project files are difficult to find because no one knows where they went.

- Personnel are reassigned and can offer only limited support to the restart effort.

- The original baseline (e.g., value proposition, doneness test, scope, and goals) may not be easily remembered or accessed.

Tactics for a successful restart (unfreezing or thawing) are like preparing fresh game meat for a future date. Instead of placing a raw loin steak unprotected into the back of the freezer, the obvious choice is to wrap or double wrap the steak in protective paper and then clearly label and place the steak into the freezer in an appropriate place for easy identification and retrieval. In the same way, successfully restarting an initiative has a lot to do with how it was frozen in the first place. Some best practices include:

Instead of placing a raw loin steak unprotected into the back of the freezer, the obvious choice is to wrap or double wrap the steak in protective paper.

- Once the decision has been made to freeze an initiative, move it from the *Now* to the *Next* list. And as in all *Next* projects, ensure an individual leader maintains accountability even though the project is inactive.

- Place a date on the initiative indicating when it is expected to be unfrozen. For example, third quarter 20XX could indicate that the initiative could be restarted. Ensure the Strategic

Improvement Roadmap also reflects this date. Review this date periodically and extend if it is not yet time. (Warning: Do not automatically thaw the initiative. Treat it like any other initiative on the *Next* list and make a formal decision to move it into *Now*, but only when the timing or circumstances are right.)

- Collect the key project materials into a central repository organized by a member of the team. If possible, have the team member write a page to summarize items such as project status, key personnel with phone numbers and locations, major accomplishments and challenges, and factors important for the restart. Make this write-up very visible so that it is the first piece of information read once the project is deemed ready to unfreeze and restart. Some clients have created a file entitled "Upon Thawing, Read Me First."

The importance of building the organizational skill of stopping, freezing, and restarting projects is that you can avoid the complexity of lower-priority items robbing the attention and energy (bandwidth capacity) of your team. It also allows you to more effectively manage your initiatives in your *Now*, *Next*, and *Monitor* lists and keep your overall plan on track.

Renewal: Managing the Portfolio Year-over-Year

Situation: The team has enjoyed success building the plan and using the SOS2ROI tools and defending against incoming for one year. But what about years two, three, four, and so on?

TACTICS FOR MAINTAINING SPEED

Several tactics will benefit teams who work with the SOS2ROI process year-over-year.

- Avoid changing the process, but instead, enhance it and get better at it. As the group gets better at managing the portfolio using *Now, Next, Monitor* (and *Stop* and *Freeze*), everyone will become more adept at the process, and you will be able to make decisions much faster, with more clarity. Some clients have used these tools for multiple years and, like driving, operated strategic management processes effortlessly throughout.

- Shake the bushes and challenge each initiative. During annual or mid-year reviews, zero-base all initiatives (temporarily put everything in *Monitor*), generate competing ideas and let each earn its way back on the *Now* and *Next* list (see chapter 9). Regularly ask, "Given what we've learned, and our changing environment and long-term goals, should we double down and place our bets on this project for another month, quarter or year?"

- Understand the opportunity for using initiatives to develop leaders and identify top talent. Because of their high-profile nature, participating in strategic initiatives can expose high-potential employees to new experiences and higher levels of management, and it can force them either to develop or to demonstrate skills not always apparent in normal venues.

Conquering Complexity and Transforming—a Serious Strategic Capability

The world, and quite possibly your organization, is fast becoming more complex. Conquering the Complexity Monster requires adaptability. In the context of strategic management and execution, it is one of the biggest challenges leaders face today. So many competing pressures vie for time and attention and claim to be the most important thing to be doing. Yet, instead of giving into the madness, leaders who understand that complexity can be conquered in many forms, reduced, and even leveraged, can embrace and not fear complexity, and learn how to become focused personally and with their teams to achieve their highest-priority goals.

Derived from necessity, and honed in the laboratory of difficult change, the SOS2ROI tool suite is an iterative approach to conquering complexity and transforming. The hope is that you will find benefit in the principles and find your own flavors of implementation to achieve your best payoff. Whether your SOS is a sinking ship or simply a big mountain to climb, embrace the process, and build a great story of improvement.

Enjoy the journey.

Chapter 12 Complexity Conqueror's Tactics:

- Accept the fact that corporate antibodies will put pressure on even the best-laid plans.

- Realize that the threat of "incoming" will be a continual challenge and that the organization will need to confront these challenges to protect priorities.

- Get great at setting priorities, and stopping and freezing existing projects to ensure priorities get the attention they deserve.

- Stop some projects, but make sure they are truly stopped. If needed, manage the psychology of the team and get them focused on new efforts.

- Freeze some projects and set them up for future success (unfreezing) when the time is *right* and you have the available bandwidth.

- Strive to become excellent at managing the portfolio of change. Keep at it until it becomes a natural act.

- Enjoy the journey.

APPENDIX

Complexity Conqueror's Tactics

Chapter 1: The Complexity Monster

- Face the reality that the Complexity Monster is lurking in your organization and is increasing in strength. You will eventually (if not soon) need to conquer this monster.

- Identify areas where organizational complexity exists, is optional, and is not adding any value. Create a plan to reduce or eliminate this complexity (Remove).

- Take stock of those aspects of complexity that are simply part of the business. Then simply acknowledge that's the reality, but don't allow it to expand (Restrain).

- Consider areas where complexity is adding value to the business. Embrace these areas and be careful not to upset the ecosystem that is encouraging that value (Reinforce).

- Continue to expand reliance on the diverse perspectives of those inside and outside your organization who, collectively, may see the complex system much more completely than you. Create a safe environment and culture where those unfiltered perspectives are increasingly accepted, allowing a more complete and accurate picture to form.

Chapter 2: The Transformation Process

- Create a means to perceive, prioritize, and manage change, both proactively and reactively. Begin to build this capability into your organization. Leaders facing complexity must become outstanding adapters.

- Prepare to learn the tactics and techniques not only to repair cracks in the business system but also enhance capabilities needed to be more competitive.

- Form a vision for the kind of culture that will succeed amidst complexity. Be sure this culture includes ways of creating openness in the organization and broadening alignment to support priorities.

Chapter 3: The Critical Mindsets

- Realize that success in strategic change goes beyond merely tools, processes, and frameworks. Mindset is critical.

- Understand the difference among green time, red time, and blue time. Strive to spend as much time as possible in the blue, and encourage team leaders to do the same.

- Plan to invest blue time to build your skills and that of your team to master the top mindsets. They don't come naturally or for free.

- Embrace the reality that to become great at change, the leader must become great at building a strong, open, and honest team that is not afraid to resolve issues, even if it's difficult or uncomfortable.

- Give yourself permission to be imperfect. Action accelerates learning, much faster than waiting.

Chapter 4: Confront the Challenge

- Take the attitude that problems are to be embraced and confronted. The complex business system is trying to communicate that something at the root needs to be addressed. Use it to gain insight and learn.

- After containing the initial circumstance, use a diverse and knowledgeable team to solve the mystery of root cause.

A diverse team has multiple perspectives and can see a much more complete view than the boss alone.

- Once the root cause is identified, plan to solve it once, completely, and forever.

- Be sure to document the rationale and the logical investigation so that others can understand and buy into the solution. This also limits future undoing.

- Always allow interpersonal, cultural, communication-oriented, and other, softer areas of the operation to be clues in the investigation.

Chapter 5: Repair the System

- Take a deep breath and embrace your responsibility to continuously improve the business system that you lead.

- Cultivate a mindset and culture that embraces issues and sees them both as sources of rare insight into your business system and as opportunities to improve.

- Understand the difference between the root cause of an issue and the system gap that caused it; solve both.

- With multiple issues, identify the one or very few that are the highest value to solve first and then solve them. Don't let up; continue until it becomes unlikely that the issue will ever occur in the future.

- Consider that most organizations realistically have the bandwidth to repair only one or two high-impact systems issues at a time.

Chapter 6: Build Capabilities

- Ensure that the organization defines a small set of clear and measurable long-term goals from which to derive capabilities.

- Consider your capability to analyze and understand the business and market environment and adapt on a regular basis.

- Use established goals and the environmental reality to drive opportunities for building enhanced capabilities that support both maintaining the current level of performance and competing at the next level.

- Resist the temptation to *always* start building capabilities from where you are today; sometimes, a teardown and new build are better than a remodel.

Chapter 7: Broaden Alignment

- Form a vision, be as specific and inspiring as possible, and let a broad group contribute to it so they "own" it.

- Think through what kind of a team is needed to achieve the vision and the long-term goals. Base it on how you score points.

- Treat off-site retreats as accelerating events (waypoints), not end-points. Use these events to accomplish a few critical tasks, avoid the laundry list, and allow plenty of time for the team to think, align and jell.

- Evaluate and prioritize opportunities for improvement in terms of how they will satisfy the vision.

- All along the way, ensure you are building alignment and commitment from the team and critical stakeholders on the overall approach, the priorities, and how to get there.

Chapter 8: Create the Plan

- Take the time to plan the highest-priority initiatives. Do it right.

- Avoid the temptation to go into too much detail too quickly. Use a three-staged approach to ensure the foundation is sound before framing the walls and hanging drywall.

- Keep the planning visible and flexible early on. Many great plans are lost forever in project management planning tools. Think in terms of five to seven major steps and twenty to thirty detailed steps (sixty max).

- Select the right leader and the right team to advise and support the initiative.

- Identify project risks and fold mitigation steps back into the plan.

- If a kickoff is required, use it to align the broader stakeholder group. Seek their ideas and get them on your side so they can help knock down inevitable barriers and cheer you on.

Chapter 9: Focus Execution

- Study the concept of management bandwidth as a constraint.

- Make a commitment to take on only the small set of changes that can be done successfully, and delay other initiatives that can or should start later.

- Adopt a three-bucket visible prioritization tool like *Now, Next, Monitor* and use it to manage the focus of the organization on priority system fixes and capability improvements.

- Facilitate a discussion with the leadership team on what items should be done *Now, Next,* or be put into *Monitor*.

- Assign someone with the responsibility to keep the *Now, Next,* and *Monitor* list fresh and accurate.

- Create a forum that meets regularly where changes to the baseline can be discussed and incorporated into the *Now, Next, Monitor* lists.

- Declare victory when an initiative is complete. Bask in the spoils and move up another item onto the *Now* list if capacity exists. Stick with it, and it will soon become a routine part of your rhythm (weekly, monthly, and quarterly).

Chapter 10: Construct the Roadmap

- Assign a small team to spend the time required to build the roadmap, including the incorporation of feedback from the broader team, stakeholders, etc.

- Keep the roadmap at a high level, showing the small set of change initiatives with title, duration, accountable leader, and start-stop expectations. Avoid the temptation to fill in too much detail, making it too complicated.

- Make the long-term objectives visible so that it is clear how the change initiatives support those objectives.

- Avoid the temptation to make your roadmap into a detailed spreadsheet. The top-level thematic view provides the sweet spot of situational thinking without getting bogged down in mechanics. It's part art and part science. Embrace the tension.

- Plan to reference the roadmap often as a backdrop for context every time you or your team communicates to stakeholders.

- Keep the roadmap visible, allowing everyone easy access to the latest version. Make it available as an online reference, place it in standard presentations, etc.

Chapter 11: Architecting the Management System

- Set up a small team or individual to administer the SOS2ROI tools (e.g., *Now, Next, Monitor, Strategic Improvement Roadmap,* and project plans for each initiative).

- Form a strategic governance council that meets regularly to review the status of the initiatives in the *Now* list, handle potential major changes, help remove roadblocks, make decisions, and move items from *Next* to *Now* (or vice versa) when appropriate.

- Set up a strategic routine with a monthly, quarterly, semiannual, and annual cycle, so that you are running your strategic improvements as a process. Mix in virtual meetings with face-to-face meetings if the team is geographically distributed.

- Install rumble strips to ensure projects don't drift off their original intent without a discussion about how the change might impact the portfolio.

- Give your team permission to stop, regroup, and make a change to an initiative if the original plan is less than ideal.

Chapter 12: Maintaining Speed

- Accept the fact that corporate antibodies will put pressure on even the best-laid plans.

- Realize that the threat of "incoming" will be a continual challenge and that the organization will need to confront these challenges to protect priorities.

- Get great at setting priorities, and stopping and freezing existing projects to ensure priorities get the attention they deserve.

- Stop some projects, but make sure they are truly stopped. If needed, manage the psychology of the team and get them focused on new efforts.

- Freeze some projects and set them up for future success (unfreezing) when the time is *right* and you have the available bandwidth.

- Strive to become excellent at managing the portfolio of change. Keep at it until it becomes a natural act.

- Enjoy the journey.

APPENDIX

Three-Stage Planning Process Questions

The following contains the expanded list of questions for the Three-Stage Planning Process for initiatives, as summarized in chapter 8.

Stage 1 Questions: Value, Doneness, and Approach

1. What is the name of the initiative?

2. What is the problem or situation?

3. What is the value proposition of the initiative? How does it tie to your vision?

4. How will you measure success?

5. What is the test of doneness (how will you know precisely when the project is complete?)

6. What is the concept and approach for accomplishing the initiative?

7. What is the scope of the initiative in terms of its major elements (or chunks)?

8. About how much will the initiative cost and how long will it take?

9. What is the low-hanging fruit that will provide a quick win?

10. Is the initiative still worth pursuing?

Stage 2 Questions: Execution, Details, and Risk

11. For each major element of this initiative, what are the four to six steps required to accomplish the element? (Repeat for each element.)

12. Who are the major stakeholders for this initiative?

13. Who could/should lead the initiative?

14. Who should be on the initiative execution team?

15. What are the major risks to accomplishing this initiative, given this approach?

16. For each major risk, what are specific mitigation steps that can be taken? (Repeat for each risk.)

17. Where can each mitigation step be folded back into details identified in #11, above?

18. Are there clear and obvious connections (dependencies) between certain actions? (Note these.)

19. What support will the team need from the boss and/or other organizations?

20. Is the initiative still worth pursuing?

Stage 3 Questions: Logistics and Team Operations

21. How much will this cost? What is the basis of estimate?

22. What are the likely funding sources?

23. What is the project duration? When will you get your first quick win?

24. How will you manage scope creep?

25. What long-lead items (e.g., processes, tools, training, staffing) could impact completion date?

26. Are there upcoming milestones or significant events that should be addressed?

27. Are there existing teams, organizations, or initiatives that can support or assist?

28. Whom do you plan to invite onto this team?

29. How often will the initiative team meet? Where? How (in-person, telephone, online meeting, etc.)? How often?

30. What are the date, time, and agenda for the first meeting?

31. Does this initiative require a formal kickoff meeting?

32. How will the team store and manage project files?

33. How and how often will a status report be sent to management and stakeholders? In what format?

34. Risk: What additional analysis must be performed?

35. Risk: Which, if any, stakeholders must be involved in providing input to the initiative?

36. What kind of focus groups or user input is needed?

37. Risk: How can the initiative be tested in smaller, limited areas (piloted) to enable learning?

38. Is the initiative still worth pursuing?

Resources

Adams, Tim. "Question Time." Editorial. *The Observer*, November 30, 2003. Accessed April 13, 2017. https://chomsky.info/interviews/20031130/.

Beaglehold, James C. *The Life of Captain James Cook*. Stanford University Press, 1974.

Beshears, John, and Francesca Gino. "Experiment with Organizational Change Before Going All In." *Harvard Business Review*. November 06, 2014. Accessed December 28, 2016. https://hbr.org/2014/10/experiment-with-organizational-change-before-going-all-in.

Collins, James C. *Good to Great: Why Some Companies Make the Leap ... and Others Don't*. New York, NY: HarperBusiness, 2001.

Dolan, George T., Arthur Miller, and James Cunningham. "There's a S.M.A.R.T Way to Write Management Goals and Objectives." *Management Review* 70, no. 11 (November 1981): 35.

Fawkes, Glynnis. The Book of Greek & Roman Folktales, Legends, & Myths. Edited by William F. Hansen. Princeton, NJ: Princeton University Press, 2017.

Kaufman, Stephen E. Sun Tzu. *The Art of War, the Definitive Interpretation of Sun Tzu's Classic Book of Strategy*. North Clarendon: Tuttle Publishing, 2001.

Katzenbach, John R., and Douglas K. Smith. "The Discipline of Teams*." Harvard Business Review*. August 25, 2015. Accessed January 04, 2017. https://hbr.org/2005/07/the-discipline-of-teams.

Lencioni, Patrick. *The Five Dysfunctions of a Team: A Leadership Fable*. San Francisco: Jossey-Bass, 2002.

Mukherjee, Siddhartha. *The* Emperor *of All Maladies*: New York, Scribner, 2010 p 38, 143

Nietzsche, Friedrich. *Beyond Good and Evil: Prelude to a Philosophy of the Future*. Edited by Rolf Peter Horstmann and Judith Norman. Cambridge: Cambridge University Press, 2016.

Porter, Michael E. *Competitive Advantage: Creating and Sustaining Superior Performance*. New York: Free Press, 2004.

Sargut, Gökçe, and Rita McGrath. "Learning to Live with Complexity." *Harvard Business Review*. October 07, 2014. Accessed April 23, 2017. https://hbr.org/2011/09/learning-to-live-with-complexity.

Schneider, Steven Jay, and Ian Haydn Smith. *1001 Movies You Must See before You Die*. Hauppage, NY: Barron's Educational Series, 2015.

Snowdon, David J., and Mary E. Boone. "A Leader's Framework for Decision Making." *Harvard Business Review*. December 07, 2015. Accessed December 23, 2016. https://hbr.org/2007/11/a-leaders-framework-for-decision-making.

Stevenson, Robert Louis. *Treasure Island*. London: Cassell and Company, 1883.

Williams, Steve. "Visualizing and Interacting with Systems." *Constructive Public Engagement*. July 29. 2013. https://constructive.net/2013/07/29/visualizing-and-interacting-with-systems/

Yeaworth, Irvin S., Director. *The Blob*. Performed by Steve McQueen. United States: Tonylyn Productions, 1958.

Acknowledgments

This book is the result of a team effort, not only during its writing but also throughout my education and career. I want to thank a few of those who have been instrumental in my journey.

Thank you to the dozens of colleagues and expert collaborators who invested time and offered insight and gentle critique to help make this book better. This includes a very special thanks to my editor, Henry DeVries, and the great team at Indie Books International—your guidance, patience, and ability to inspire through stories is a true asset and a gift.

To my parents, who never had a doubt: Thank you for consistently offering me your best advice, trusting my abilities, and being your best example, whether your vantage point was near or far.

To my siblings, Carey, Michael, Steven, and Julia: Your humor, support, and commitment to always stand by my family and me are forever appreciated.

To my kids, Matt, Scot, and Kate: Watching you growing up so (darn) fast is amazing, albeit providing more than a few SOS moments for me. You have taught me to slice trivial from timeless. It's an honor to be walking with you.

To the clients of Global Aperture over our first decade of business, for trusting us to stand with you in times of challenge, and celebrate with you in times of triumph: It's a pleasure to help you create your best day.

To my assistant of ten years, Marilyn Christensen: Thank you for anticipating my every move, being awesome where I'm not, and for always encouraging the team and me to strive.

To the team at Global Aperture, past and present: Your patience, expertise, and commitment have helped us serve our clients with heart, and has made me a better professional and leader. A special thank you to Dave Whelan. I continue to marvel at your "pattern recognizing" superpowers, and I appreciate all the battles we've waged over the past decade.

To Col. Robert P. Lyons Jr. (USAF–Retired), whose charge to me as a young officer to "assume any and all authority not specifically denied" has encouraged me to push harder and take more risks: Thank you.

To Craig Whaley, Columbine High School coach and teacher, for your words of encouragement on November 21, 1986: Although you may not remember what you said, I do.

To Frank DeAngelis, Columbine High School coach, teacher, and eventual principal who faced that SOS moment that rocked our community and nation, for making good on your fifteen-year promise that even the elementary school kids that day would have a chance to graduate safely on your watch: I am stirred by your example.

To the men and women in uniform, past, present, and future: Thank you for your willingness to pay the ultimate price so we could be free.

And foremost, to the One who put it all on the line so I could be free.

As an aside:

When I asked my ten-year-old daughter what to write in the About the Author section, she suggested, "Say that you are a good Dad."

I said, "Thanks, I appreciate that."

She replied, "I appreciate that, too."

Pretty cool.

About the Author

Larry Haas is the Founder and CEO of Global Aperture Inc., a management consulting firm specializing in helping organizations improve and transform to achieve their strategic goals.

As a consultant, Larry's work has spanned a cross-section of functional areas in industries such as Aerospace and Defense, Agriculture, Business Services, Corrections, Food and Beverage, Homeland Security, and Nonprofits.

Clients and colleagues often refer to Larry's sixth-sense ability to see into situations to clarify the complicated and conquer the complex. This ability has consistently provided more boldness for leaders and clearly defined action for teams and operational and financial impact for organizations.

Prior to founding Global Aperture, Larry served as a consultant and leader in organizations such as Procter and Gamble, Deloitte, Diamond Technology Partners (now part of PricewaterhouseCoopers), The Boeing Company, and as an officer and program manager in the United States Air Force.

Larry is a Hall of Fame alumnus of Columbine High School in Littleton, Colorado, received his BS in Aerospace Engineering from the University of Arizona, and his MBA with an emphasis in finance and strategy from the UCLA Anderson school.

Larry lives in the Los Angeles area with his two sons, Matthew ("Matt") and Scot, and his daughter, Kate.

To learn more about Larry and Global Aperture, please visit www. globalaperture.com.

Made in the USA
San Bernardino, CA
25 August 2017